MW01102030

HELL *and*
High Water:

An Assessment
of Paul Martin's
Record and
Implications
for the Future

Edited by Todd Scarth

Hell *and* High Water

An assessment of Paul Martin's record and implications for the future

Edited by Todd Scarth

National Library of Canada Cataloguing in Publication

Hell *and* high water: an assessment of Paul Martin's record and implications for the future / edited by Todd Scarth.

Includes bibliographical references.

ISBN 0-88627-363-3

1. Martin, Paul, 1938- 2. Canada – Politics and government – 1993-

3. Canada – Economic policy – 1991- 4. Canada – Social policy. I. Scarth, Todd II. Canadian Centre for Policy Alternatives.

FC636.M37H44 2004   971.064'8'092   C2004-901331-9

Cover design by Studio 2 studio2@rogers.com

Book layout by Nadene Rehnby www.handsonpublications.com

Canadian Centre for Policy Alternatives
Suite 410, 75 Albert Street
Ottawa, ON K1P 5E7
Tel 613-563-1341 Fax 613-233-1458
www.policyalternatives.ca
ccpa@policyalternatives.ca

Contents

About the authors

John Anderson is Research Director with the Canadian Council on Social Development.

Bruce Campbell is the Executive Director of the CCPA.

Joe Gunn is the Director of Social Affairs with the Canadian Conference of Catholic Bishops.

Andrew Jackson is a Senior Economist with the Canadian Labour Congress.

Hugh Mackenzie is an economist and a CCPA Research Associate.

Dale Marshall is a Research Fellow with the CCPA. He recently accepted a position at the David Suzuki Foundation.

Todd Scarth is Director of the CCPA's Manitoba office.

Jim Stanford is a Senior Economist with the Canadian Auto Workers.

Cindy Wiggins is a senior health and social policy researcher with the Canadian Labour Congress.

Armine Yalnizyan is an economist and Senior Research Fellow with the CCPA.

One Good Story, That One
Paul Martin's Policy Legacy

by Todd Scarth

Who is Paul Martin? On one level, the story is by now numbingly familiar. Martin is The Man Who Killed the Deficit. He is the knight who slew the dragon, the sheriff who ran the desperado out of town. It is almost the stuff of a Hollywood movie or popular legend, although, this being Canadian politics, the villain was neither dragon nor alien invader nor evil genius, but a federal budgetary calculation. Still, as these things go, it was a heroic feat, this wrestling the deficit to the ground, and at the same time it was distinctly humble and matter-of-fact. After all, Martin was simply demanding of a bloated, unresponsive government that it do what ordinary families had to do as a matter of course: balance the books. Perhaps the ultimate proof of his fiscal straight shooting was that, before long, he had the government beating its own budget projections every single year, year after year.

It really is a good story.

But does Martin's reputation as fiscal savior hold up to scrutiny? What are the real implications of his policy legacy? This book sets out to answer these questions by examining critically the policy decisions Martin made in Finance, and his influence, both direct and indirect, on other portfolios, in the ten full years since bringing down his first budget. And it does so with an eye to projecting where he will take the country in the future.

When Jean Chrétien announced his first cabinet, the two men seen as his strongest potential rivals for the leadership of the Liberals were given what at the time were widely seen as kiss-of-death portfolios. Lloyd Axworthy was handed the task of overhauling massive federal human resources programs, including the one he would soon gut and rename Employment Insurance. Paul Martin, of course, took over Finance, and with it the task of bringing the federal budget into balance. Because of the painful spending cuts each of these ministers would be expected to implement, they were not unlike political sappers, trying to defuse bombs that could blow up their political careers – or, at the very least, their leadership ambitions.

Axworthy, a holdout from the party's shrinking left wing, acknowledged the awkwardness of his position, and the contradictions he faced in trying to achieve some sort of progressive reform when his real job was simply to cut. This approach, while perhaps intellectually satisfying, was politically ham-fisted – imagine *The English Patient's* Kip looking up from an important clutch of brightly coloured wires to deliver a digressive lecture on the history of gunpowder – and, kaboom, human resources reform exploded in his face. While he shook off this ignominy and went on to serve with distinction as Minister of Foreign Affairs, it has been years since Axworthy – now back where he started at the University of Winnipeg (though this time as President) – was considered Liberal leadership material.

Martin's approach could not have been more different from Axworthy's. After pausing to get his bearings with his first budget, he embraced the challenge of spending cuts, turning the war on the deficit into a crusade, with himself as leader. His achievement of converting the usual political quagmire of Finance into a platform that established him as Chrétien's clear successor – much to Chrétien's chagrin – allowed him to win the Liberal leadership with more than 90% of the vote. His political and strategic brilliance cannot be questioned.

Which is not to say that there are no questions to be asked.

For example, consider Martin's reputation as the one responsible for whipping the federal budget into shape. As Jim Stanford demonstrates in his essay in this book, Martin's reputation is as "rose coloured" as were the budget projections of his predecessors that he so effectively criticized. While the deficit did need to be brought under control, Martin, with strong support from the business and financial communities, did so more quickly and much more painfully than necessary. And, rather than an act of fiscal prudence, the practice he established of deliberately and dramatically low-balling budget projections was a tawdry shell game designed to perpetu-ate historically low levels of program spending long after any fiscal justifi-cation for it had gone. Stanford reveals some of the significant errors made on Martin's watch.

After several painful years, the deficit disappeared quickly. (So quickly, in fact, that it calls into question how serious the problem really was in the first place.) Once it was gone, Martin faced a political challenge: Canadi-ans had not supported the program cuts of the 1990s for the sake of pro-gram cuts. In their chapters, Armine Yalnizyan and Hugh Mackenzie ex-plain how Martin solved this problem by using taxation policy and the war on "big government" to reduce the federal government's capacity to raise the revenue needed to re-invest in the programs that had been sacrificed in the deficit fight. By 2002-03, federal spending was down to 11.5% of GDP, a rate last seen in 1949-50, a time before the creation of most of the major social programs Canadians benefit from today.

Obviously, spending cannot be cut that low without programs suffering, and the program sacrifices that Canadians were forced to make are detailed throughout this book.

In the second half of the 1990s, Mar-tin triggered a process in which govern-ments across the country systematically offloaded responsibility for services onto lower levels of government. The federal government cut transfers to the provinces, which in turn tightened the screws on municipalities. While federal surpluses are now commonplace, municipal infrastructure crum-bles, and local school boards, at the bottom of the hierarchy, have to scram-ble and increase taxes to make up for provincial education cuts.

Does Martin's reputation as fiscal savior hold up to scrutiny? What are the real implications of his policy legacy? This book sets out to answer these questions.

While the effects of the cuts of the 1990s rippled down from the fed-eral level to the local, the backlash could move in reverse. Public unhappi-ness with poor services, beginning at the ground level (literally, in the case of failing roads and sewers), will return like an boomerang. The blame will move in reverse, eventually hitting Martin directly. And he will be doubly vulnerable, as he made himself the public face of the cuts.

An added difficulty for Martin is that he is now going it alone, without the humanizing – and teflon-coated – presence of Jean Chrétien.

Even while the money is there, Martin has made it clear that no one should expect the services to be there. This would appear to be his personal priority, and in any case his political positioning leaves him little choice. Martin is constrained not only on spending, but also when it comes to stimulative fiscal policy. The boom of the late 1990s and early in the new century owes a good deal to the low-interest rate policy of the Bank of Canada, and a fortuitous combination of a low dollar and the mighty American consumer. We also had the good fortune that, even as the U.S. economy began to slump under the Bush administration, two key exports – cars and lumber – remained relatively recession-proof. The Canadian macro-economy, in other words, has enjoyed a run of good luck that cannot continue forever. Yet the counter-cyclical spending and prudent short-term deficits that will be needed to stimulate growth may, in an era of "hell-or-high water" balanced budgets, seem politically out or reach. When the expectation is that federal finances will beat expectations, Martin will find he has very little room to manoeuvre.

As Prime Minister, Martin's first crisis erupted from the Auditor-General's revelations of corruption and the misspending of $100 million in the Quebec sponsorship debacle. But his most significant challenge may turn out to be his own legacy as Finance Minister. This is equally true of popular perception, for politicians who live by the story die by the story. The line that separates firmness, prudence, and determination from stubbornness, inflexibility, and meanness is thin, and, if he does not have what it takes to repair much of the damage that he caused since his first budget in 1994, Martin will find himself on the wrong side of that line.

—*Todd Scarth*

CHAPTER 1

Paul Martin's
Permanent Revolution

by Armine Yalnizyan

In his quest to deliver small government to Canadians, Paul Martin created a revolution in how the federation works. His reign as the federal Finance Minister brought about lasting change in three ways: shrinking the scope and role of government, neutering funding mechanisms, and deeply cutting spending, even for programs the government was committed to providing. These changes transformed relations between federal, provincial, and municipal governments, profoundly decentralizing decision-making and balkanizing public provision. It also transformed the budgetary process, making surpluses, not deficits, the norm.

From the outset of the revolution to his taking over as Prime Minister, Paul Martin has been consistent in saying he wanted this approach to governance to be permanent, inalterable. From 1995 through 1999 he cut spending, and in 2000 he locked in these changes through tax cuts and debt repayment, soaking up surpluses to restrict the possibility of significant re-expansion in government spending. By late 2003, though Paul Martin's rhetoric was starting to lean leftward towards social investments, the specifics were about lower taxes and more aggressive debt repayment.

Now, as The Man Who Killed Big Government takes over the leadership of the federal government, the permanency of his small government revolution is in question. An unprecedented string of budgetary surpluses continues side by side with a struggling health care system and crumbling infrastructure for water, roads, electricity, schools and hospitals – making it obvious that, even when the resources are there, the basics are not guaranteed. Has the public's reduced expectation of government become a lasting feature of Canadian politics or will Canadians ultimately demand a more sustainable approach to governance? Can Paul Martin remain a hero without moving away from the cold comfort of small government?

Tracing the source of the "revolution"

To a very great degree, Paul Martin owes his credentials as a political leader to the dexterity with which he caught and surfed the wave of small government as it crashed over Canada in the 1990s.

The idea was not his. Its ascent can be traced to the Washington Consensus – a convergence of thought in the IMF (International Monetary Fund), the World Bank, and the U.S. Federal Reserve. The consensus was about "rethinking" the role of the state by testing just how much the market can replace the state's function. It emerged in response to the dual crises of the 1970s: economic stagnation in developed nations and the increasing demand for economic development by Third World nations.

The reasoning went like this: by scaling back the role of the state, we can make more room for the market to do what it's ostensibly good at – making money. Less government leads to more market, which leads to more money, which leads to more prosperity and, ostensibly, reduced poverty. The moral underpinning is that this circuit leads to more prosperity *for all*, at least in theory. Who could be against that?

By the 1980s, the Washington Consensus had codified the elements of what could propel a nation into this virtuous circle. By the 1990s, the recipe for revitalizing economic growth has become a one-size-fits-all formula for developing and developed nations alike: increase the economy's export-orientation and reliance on trade; cut program spending and public investments; improve the climate for business investments, including cutting taxes; and place more priority on deficit/debt reduction.

This approach was well underway when Paul Martin took over the reins of Canada's Finance Ministry, and brought the concept of small government to fruition in Canada with the zeal of a revolutionary. Deficit reduction provided the rationale to reduce the size of government operations to a historically unprecedented degree. Paul Martin bragged about the scale of the cuts, wearing his accomplishments-to-come like a badge of honour.

> ...[O]ver the next three fiscal years, this budget will deliver cumulative savings of $29 billion, of which $25.3 billion are expenditure cuts. This is by far the largest set of actions in any Canadian budget since demobilization after the Second World War... Relative to the size of our economy, program spending will be lower in 1996-97 than at any time since 1951.

Paul Martin's Budget speech, February 1995, page 4

> Our reductions in government expenditure are unprecedented in modern Canadian history... Our reform of the role of government offers the prospect of much more effective government at substantially lower cost... Constant renewal is what this country is all about. Indeed, it is the essential ingredient of a dynamic federalism.

Ibid. p.25

The heroic language of the Budget Speech was disingenuous in two regards: the comparison with the federal government's post-war efforts, and the significance of small government.

It ignored the fact that the initiatives of the 1995 budget were about to undo key elements of what had painstakingly been built since the Second World War. The post-war effort was about growth – which, in those days, meant building a nation through increased public expenditures and investments. The 1995 Paul Martin budget was about cuts – but more than just a reduction in spending, these initiatives represented a collapse of both federal supports and national vision. It redefined growth to represent the interests of the market, rather than the interests of the nation.

Looking at the future through the rear view mirror

Using 1951 as a benchmark of success may illustrate the inner logic of the Paul Martin approach to budget-making, but this comparison to half a century ago, again, is deeply misleading.

While Martin slashed the level of program spending as a share of the economy to what it was in 1951, there are fundamental differences between what the federal government did in the 1950s and what it did in the

1990s. The federal government of the 1950s did not provide programs such as Medicare or a comprehensive system of elderly benefits. Those social gains were only won after prolonged campaigns on the part of civil society. Nor did the federal government of the 1950s face chronically high unemployment rates. Unemployment rates in the 1990s were more than double the rates of the post-war period, putting pressures on governments on both sides of the ledger: more income supports flowing out, less income tax paid in.

The "actions" of the 1995 budget altered the political landscape through massive cuts and the privatization of public services. By 2002-03, federal spending was down to 11.5% of GDP, a rate last seen in 1949-50. The clock was being turned further back than 1951.

Paul Martin took over the reins of Canada's Finance Ministry, and brought the concept of small government to fruition in Canada with the zeal of a revolutionary.

The scale of withdrawal of federal funds has triggered cascading devolution, from federal to provincial governments, from provincial to municipal governments. Downloading was accompanied by off-loading, shifting services from public to private provision, or eliminating services. The impact of these changes regionalized the federation, created growing inequalities between and within regions, and threw the nation's major urban centres into disarray as they struggled to do more with less help from the more senior levels of government.

Instead of building a nation, Paul Martin's battle plan was taking it apart.

Make it permanent

One revolutionary aspect of this massive downsizing was the notion that no program was *a priori* a fundamental element of the public good. Everything was up for review, and could be classified as no longer "core" to the mission and purpose of government. The utility of all government functions would henceforth be subject to institutionalized review, a permanent feature of the new era ushered in by Martin.

> *Let me just say one thing before leaving Program Review, and that is, we have accomplished much, but getting government right does not end*

with this budget. For the essence of good government is, in fact, permanent ongoing program review. And that is our intention...If government doesn't need to run something, it shouldn't. And in the future, it won't.

Paul Martin's Budget speech, February 1995, page 14

Martin's Program Review cut the departments of transportation, regional development, and natural resources by half. The biggest cuts, in dollar amounts, came from HRDC (Human Resource Development Canada, which was cut by more than a third), Transport, and Defence/Emergency Preparedness. Business subsidies were cut by 60% – to be replaced by sizeable tax cuts. Program Review also raised money through cost-recovery in departments that did not previously charge fees for public service or by revenue generation through privatizing those activities.

Downloading the revolution

Relations with the provinces were unilaterally changed with the introduction of the Canada Health and Social Transfer – a potent symbol of the permanent revolution.

The CHST combined two previous funding mechanisms into a single pot of money with fewer conditions on how to meet a range of social needs, from health care and post-secondary education to social services and social assistance. The loss of conditions most affected supports to the poor, who lost what weak guarantees for support that had previously existed. This new incarnation of unconditional federal support was kicked off with a $7 billion cut in funds transferred to the provinces for these programs. The reason given for the cuts was that the provinces needed more flexibility, especially with regard to welfare programs. Under the logic of small government, guaranteed funding was too "restrictive."

...[W]e believe that the restrictions attached by the federal government to transfer payments in areas of clear provincial responsibility should be minimized. At present, transfers under the Canada Assistance Plan come with a lot of unnecessary strings attached. They limit the flexibility of the provinces to innovate. They increase administrative costs. In short, the cost-sharing approach of the past no longer helps the provinces, who have clear responsibility to design and deliver social assistance programs, to do so in a way that is as effective as possible and in tune with local needs.

Budget speech 95 p17

In reality, Martin burdened the provinces with the most restrictive tool of all: funding cuts. The provinces were left to decide whether they would maintain service levels in these programs or offload costs by downloading services to municipalities, by reducing quality or access to services, or by letting the market decide who gets what based on a person's ability to pay. This exacerbated the already existing balkanization of services, with provinces using the loss of funds and the loss of conditionality of federal funding as their rationale to reduce or offload service provision. It was truly a step back in time.

Cities feel the impact of downloading

Many public provisions, including social housing, were simply abandoned. By the end of the 1990s, the mayors of the biggest cities from coast to coast found themselves overwhelmed by the magnitude of the mismatch between supply and demand at the low end of the housing market. The widespread inadequacy of affordable shelter and the growing ranks of the homeless brought to mind the Great Depression, and just like during Dirty Thirties, the mayors descended on Ottawa in 1998, proclaiming a "National Housing Disaster," begging federal Finance Minister Paul Martin for some support and relief. The plea went unanswered, though it was heard by a great listener.

The revolutionary principles of small government came first, as Paul Martin was apt to say, "come hell or high water."

As with other impassioned supplications for infrastructure maintenance – secure potable water, public transit, reduction of child poverty, early child education, and environmental protections – Martin responded with sympathy and encouragement: the need was real, the cause was great. But, despite record financial prosperity in the late 1990s, he was never able to move forward. He would if he could, he would perpetually assure the supplicants, but the cupboard was perpetually bare. The revolutionary principles of small government came first, as Paul Martin was apt to say, "come hell or high water."

The following retrospective on Paul Martin's decade of revolution offers a "program review" of sorts. It reviews how the agenda of small government/ big business played itself out in the period 1993 to 2002. These include: spending cuts; increased reliance on trade and foreign investment; cuts in inflation and borrowing costs; tax cuts; and debt repayment. What has been the impact of the revolution, and can it be permanent?

The defining features of the "small government" revolution

1. REDUCE THE SIZE OF GOVERNMENT

Among the G-7 nations, Canada implemented the most aggressive reduction in the size of government over the 1990s.[1] Federal program spending shrank by 30% between 1993-94 and 2000-01, from 15.7% of GDP to 11% of GDP.[2] In 2002-03, federal program spending increased to 11.5%, but this was more than half a percentage point lower than what the government allocated in the 2002 budget, a shortfall in promised spending of $5.2 billion. This may be symptomatic of future budgets, as the Finance Minister of the day, John Manley, indicated:

> There are many reasons that our surplus last year was higher than projected. But one reason was that our program spending was lower than budgeted. That's a good sign and a portent for the future.
>
> Economic and Fiscal Update, October 29, 2003, page 7

The 2003 budget – under a new Finance Minister – simply shows how permanent the Martin commitment to small government has become. It said there would be a small bump-up in spending due to renewed investments in health care, raising the spending to GDP ratio to 12.2%. As seen above, though increased investments in health care took place, other spending did not, leaving the ratio at 11.5%, a rate last seen in 1949-50.

The 2003 budget shows that the ratio of program spending to GDP is projected to continue its downward trajectory after the 2002-03 fiscal year. It promises to not exceed 12% of GDP over the next two years.[3] One can only wonder if this means a commitment to not exceed the 11.5% mark.

Paul Martin's Program Review is now permanently institutionalized. A central feature of the Martin budgets right up to 2002, Budget 2003 states:

> To demonstrate its commitment to reallocating spending and improving efficiency, the Government will reallocate $1 billion from existing spending beginning in 2003–04 to fund higher government priorities. This reallocation will be permanent and represent about 15% of the cost of the new initiatives announced in this budget over the next two years...
> As part of its ongoing review of programs, the Treasury Board will continue to examine the scope for reallocating from lower to higher priorities and may adjust departmental and agency budgets accordingly.
>
> The Budget Plan 2003, Page 177

2. INCREASE RELIANCE ON TRADE

The key policy initiative for economic growth since the mid-1980s has been to increase Canada's openness to trade, particularly making economic production more export- oriented. Canadian exports have more than doubled since. Exports rose as a share of the economy, from 26% in 1990 to almost half the economy's output in 2001 (45.6%). During this time, the U.S. share of total Canadian exports grew from 74% in 1990 to around 87% since 1999, making the government's strategy of export orientation even more vulnerable to economic conditions in the U.S.[4]

Between 1990 and 2002, exports more than doubled, from $175 billion to $473 billion. The value of exports peaked in the first quarter of 2001, at $512 billion. The U.S. remains the most important market for our exports, accounting for 87.4% of all Canadian merchandise exports in 2002.[5] Since the events of 9/11, a slowing economic climate globally, and with a strengthening Canadian dollar, exports declined to 38% of the economy by the second quarter of 2003.

Imports followed the same pattern, more than doubling from $175 billion in 1990 to $429 billion in 2000, then declining to $408 billion by the second quarter of 2003. Whereas Canadians imported more than they exported a decade ago, today the relationship is reversed.

3. ATTRACT MORE FOREIGN INVESTMENT

Foreign direct investment in Canada (inward FDI) grew dramatically in the 1990s, from $130 billion in 1990 to $292 billion in 2000, and to $349 billion by 2002[6]. Two-thirds of this flow came from the United States. As a share of the economy, inward FDI grew from 19.6% of GDP in 1990 to 30% of GDP by 2002. Compared to other G-7 nations, the Canadian economy is highly open to foreign investment: the G-7 average over the same period also grew, but from 6.3% of GDP to 13.6% of GDP.[7]

Canadian investors are also spending more overseas. Since 1990, outward FDI from Canadian companies grew by more than four times, to reach $432 billion in 2002.[8] Clearly the growing reliance on foreign capital is not due to Canada's ability to generate its own capital for the purposes of investment.

4. LOWER INFLATION, LOWER THE COSTS OF BORROWING

Starting in 1990, the primary objective of the Bank of Canada has been to reduce inflation and maintain it in the target range of 1% and 3%. The Bank has been highly successful. Canada's annual inflation rate averaged 1.7% between 1993 and 2002, one of the lowest in the G-7 countries.[9] This vies with only two other protracted periods of low inflation in Canada: from 1934 through to the end of the Second World War, and from 1952 to 1965.[10]

While the costs of borrowing also dropped dramatically over the 1990s, the economic slowdown – which started in 2001 and was exacerbated by the events of 9/11 in New York – triggered a series of interest rate cuts over the course of 2001 which were unparalleled in the central bank's history. In January 2002, the Bank of Canada set the prime lending rate for business at 3.75%, the lowest nominal rate in our history.[11] The previous low was between November 1944 and March 1956, when interest rates were set to service the economy at 4.5%. The prime rate has been 4.5% since September 2003.

The Results

1. A VASTLY LARGER ECONOMY. . .

From 1993 to halfway through 2003, the Canadian economy grew by 66% in nominal terms and 41% in inflation-adjusted terms.[12] By half-way through 2003, Canadians were producing $1.2 trillion in goods and services. This is $480 billion more on an annual basis than a decade before, and growing. There is vastly greater capacity to finance social development initiatives, should that be a political priority.

2. BUT WE'RE MOVING FURTHER AWAY FROM COVERING THE HUMAN BASICS

At the same time, the cuts that took place mean virtually all social development initiatives to cover the human basics identified in the 1948 Universal Declaration of Human Rights – clean water, shelter, food, health care and education – are increasingly in jeopardy for growing numbers of Canadians. Though there is more economic capacity to meet these needs than at any other time in our history, there are fewer resources devoted to these purposes. The aggressive redistribution of resources has resulted in unprecedented wealth coinciding with the following miserable facts in our nation:

Deepening Poverty

The proportion of families defined as poor decreased from 1996 to 2001 from 14% to 10.4% of all Canadians. However, there are more poor children today (786,000) than in 1989 (765,000), the year when a campaign to eliminate child poverty was unanimously endorsed by all parties in the federal Parliament.[13] Furthermore, the depth of poverty continues to increase among those who remain defined as poor. The average low-income family would now require more than an additional $7,200 in after-tax dollars to reach the "low-income" threshold. In 1995, it would have taken $6,800.[14] Young men's earnings have not returned to the levels of the 1980s, in inflation-adjusted terms, although single female parents continue to improve their economic position by getting more employment and working longer hours.

Poverty is more prevalent for the single elderly, the disabled, visible minorities, Aboriginal populations (both on and off reserve) and recent immigrants; and in all these groups women are the most disadvantaged.

Inequality (in market and in after-tax terms) has grown more rapidly since 1995 than at any other time since records have been kept. The top 20% of families were, on average, five-and-a-half times more affluent than the bottom 20% of families after taxes and transfers were taken into account. From the 1970s to 1995, the relationship between rich and poor was somewhat stable, the top 20% of families averaging $4.80 for every $1 in after-tax income of the bottom 20%.[15]

More People Precariously Housed, More Homeless

A high proportion of families spend a disproportionate amount of their income on rent. In 2001, almost 20% of Canadian renters paid *more than half* of their income towards shelter costs. Forty percent paid more than 30% of their income toward shelter.[16]

Between 1991 and 2001, Ontario – which houses almost 40% of Canada's population – lost 24,300 existing rental units. Not surprisingly, rents have been rising at twice the inflation rate.[17]

While there are no official statistics on the number of homeless, it has been reported that about 250,000 people will be without shelter over the course of the year.[18] In Toronto alone, 44 homeless people died – most from exposure – in 2001. By the middle of 2003, Toronto's regular vigils for the homeless mourned the deaths of 308 people.

More Hunger

The first food bank opened in Canada in 1981. By 2003 there were at least 639 food banks, with an additional 2,213 agencies helping hungry people across the country, more than the number of MacDonald's outlets in the country.[19]

With rising rents and stagnant or falling incomes, the squeeze-play for too many households has resulted in increased hunger. Food bank use has reached 778,000 people in one month alone, and has doubled since 1989. More than 40% of the users are children. Every year, whether the economy is booming or slowing, the use of food banks increases. Just since 2002, the number of people in food bank lines has risen by 5.5%. The CAFB (Canadian Association of Food Banks) survey shows that 12.9% of food bank users are people with jobs. An astounding 7.03 million pounds of food is distributed in one month, but shelves are often bare at month's end.[20]

> With rising rents and stagnant or falling incomes, the squeeze-play for too many households has resulted in increased hunger.

Insecure Access to
Clean Drinking Water

Poor maintenance of infrastructure and the intensification of agri-pro-duction has resulted in more frequent instances of unsafe drinking water in communities from coast to coast. In 2001, 7,000 people were infected by a cryptosporidiosis outbreak in North Battleford, Saskatchewan; half the 500 communities in Newfoundland had a boil-water advisory during the summer; and one of the biggest cities in the country (Vancouver) is-sued a water safety warning to its residents in early 2002. These most recent developments occurred despite the fact that, in 2000, seven people died and thousands became seriously ill in Walkerton, Ontario, when E-coli found its way into the water system. The report of the public inquiry into Walkerton, released in January 2002, cited two factors as the cause of this debacle: the incompetence of local authorities and funding cutbacks by the provincial government to its Environmental Protection branch.[21]

Rising Student Debt, Decreased Returns on Investments in Education

Funding to post-secondary education has still not been restored to the pre-cut levels despite historic budgetary surpluses. These cuts, combined with deregulation of fees, have resulted in large tuition increases, with fee increases for professional schools only limited by what the market will bear. On average, students completing a four-year program will have $25,000 in debt, an increase of 300% from 1990.[22]

Shifting job opportunities mean the returns on investment in post-secondary credentials may be uncertain, especially among the growing number of young graduates who are precariously employed. According to the 2001 Census, half of all employed Canadians between 25 and 35 years of age earned less than $26,822 in 2000. Their average annual income was $29,876. (The average Canadian worker earned $31,757 in 2000, while median earnings – the half-way point of all workers' earnings – was $25,052.)[23]

Rising Problems of Access to Health Care

Canada has one of the lowest doctor-to-population ratios in the Western world: 2.1 doctors for every 1,000 patients.[24] Labour shortages among health professionals is a global problem, but was exacerbated in Canada by reductions to enrolment in medical and nursing schools in the 1990s in order to deal with funding cutbacks – cuts that originated with the federal government.

The result is that, in 2003, 3 million Canadians do not have a family doctor[25], overburdening acute care services such as emergency rooms and keeping waiting lists for diagnostics and treatment stubbornly high. Almost one in five Canadians requiring health care for themselves or a family member in 2001 encountered some form of difficulty in gaining access to services.[26]

The one harsh lesson from the small government revolution is: Economic growth does not necessarily lead to prosperity for all. It requires political will to ensure that "more prosperity for all" is an explicit objective, so that it can be an outcome of economic growth, through more jobs with better wages and working conditions and more abundant social provisions.

3. RECORD BUDGETARY SURPLUSES AT THE FEDERAL LEVEL

There is no reason for such hardship in Canada. This nation has outperformed all other G-7 nations in GDP growth since 1993. What have we done with all this new wealth?

Continued constraints on federal public spending, combined with relatively strong economic conditions, resulted in the fiscal year 2002-03 as the sixth consecutive year in which the federal government recorded a budget surplus. This feat has only been accomplished once before, in the six-year period immediately after World War II, 1946-57 to 1951-02.

The scale of the current surpluses has, however, not previously been seen. The growing size of the surplus created enormous pressure to make it disappear before Canadians started to expect more from their governments. If the small government revolution was to be permanent, the cupboard had to *appear* bare.

By October 2000, the solution was to introduce an explicit and aggressive tax cut agenda and accelerate the campaign of vigorous debt repayment. In the build-up to the federal election in November 2000, calculations of the projected size of the federal budget surplus over the following five-year horizon ranged between $150 billion and almost $200 billion.[27] Most of this ($100 billion) was devoted to tax cuts. Debt reduction, until recently, has never been an explicit objective of this government – yet the second largest amount turned out to be debt repayment, not program spending ($52 billion in debt repayment since 1997-98, of which only $18 billion had been paid down by the time of the October 2000 announcements).[28]

> The growing size of the surplus created enormous pressure to make it disappear before Canadians started to expect more from their governments. If the small government revolution was to be permanent, the cupboard had to *appear* bare.

Lock in the Change

1. DEEP TAX CUTS

The federal government's initiatives in the October 2000 *Economic Statement and Budget Update* outlined a program for $100 billion in tax cuts over the next five years as the key way of distributing and eliminating the projected budgetary surplus.

Tax cuts in 2000-01, the first fiscal year of the plan, cost federal coffers $7 billion. That cost rose to $16 billion in 2001-02 and to $20.5 billion in 2002-03. The projected costs of the final two years of these tax cuts would reduce federal revenues by $25 billion in 2003-04 and $31 billion in 2004-05. If anything, these projections, made in mid-2000, underestimate the value of these cuts, and the ones that have been added in budgets since

2000. The federal government has not publicly kept track of the growing cost of the tax cut agenda to the public purse.

Even the events of 9/11 and the deepening economic slowdown would not alter government commitments to tax cuts – even as Canadians began to question the wisdom of permanently small governments.

The federal Finance Ministers, both Martin and his successor John Manley, have repeated that, although downturns may result in cuts to other programs, the promise to reduce taxes by $100 billion remains sacrosanct. Indeed, these cuts have been augmented, with the elimination of the capital tax on corporations and raising the tax-exempt threshold for RRSP (Registered Retirement Savings Plans) contributions, a move that benefits only those earning more than $75,000 a year. The implications of those cuts have not been fully costed in budget documents.[29] Budget 2003 introduced these and other tax cuts, the total of which will cost an additional $2.3 billion by 2004-05.[30] Martin's recent speeches indicate that still more tax cuts lie ahead.

Together, the federal and provincial governments have forgone at least $40 billion in revenues in 2002-03, $48 billion in 2003-04, and $61 billion in 2004-05, making tax cuts a far greater priority of governments than any other initiative in this period.

2. REDUCE THE DEBT

Net federal public debt fell from a high of 68.4% of GDP in 1995-96 to 44.2% of GDP in 2002-03, the fastest and deepest rate of reduction within the G-7 nations.[31]

Between 1996-97 and 2002-03, Canada's public debt was reduced by $52.3 billion, making debt reduction the second biggest priority (behind tax cuts) in new spending since the late 1990s.[32] A record $17.1 billion was paid by the federal government in the 2000-01 fiscal year alone, which Finance Minister Paul Martin called "the real fiscal dividend" of the budgetary surplus.

The good news about a rapidly falling debt-to-GDP ratio is that Canadians taxpayers spend less on servicing the debt than before. In the 1995-06 fiscal year, 37 cents of every tax dollar received by the federal government went to debt charges. By 2002-03, it was only 23 cents on the dollar. That translates into many billions of dollars in freed-up resources. In 2002-03, alone, the Budget estimates public debt charges will fall by $2.1 billion.[33]

But, even when significant "new" resources are available for other priorities, that doesn't guarantee the money will be spent on enhancing public provisions. Just as in a household budget, the "windfall" could go to more spending or paying off debt. In the case of the government, however, there is a third choice of where the money could go – lowering taxes.

Prudent Choices?

One of the most common, though not most heroic, words in Paul Martin's lexicon is "prudent."

Low-balling revenues and under-spending budgetary allocations is prudent. Contingency reserves for the unforeseen event is prudent. Debt repayment is prudent.

Indeed, all these things would be prudent, even admirable, in a household budget.

But no household would pay off the mortgage while the foundation of the house crumbled, the pipes threatened to burst, and someone was going hungry or without enough winter clothes. Certainly, no household would launch on such an undertaking while, at the same time, volunteering to get paid a lower hourly rate.

> No household would pay off the mortgage while the foundation of the house crumbled, the pipes threatened to burst, and someone was going hungry or without enough winter clothes.

That is, however, exactly what the Government of Canada has been doing. It has been aggressively paying off the debt while watching the deterioration of our road and transit systems, water and sewage systems, and the existing stock of public housing, hospitals and schools. It has held the line on spending while paying down the debt, knowing that Canadian children and adults go hungry and even die from lack of shelter. And, at the same time that it decided to tackle the more than $500 billion in debt – half a *trillion* dollars – it has chosen to forgo significant amounts of its own income by cutting some tax rates and entirely eliminating others. And the game is about to escalate.

Moving the Goal Posts of Success

The ratio of debt-to-GDP has taken on a new gravitas as the leading indicator of economic success for the federal government. Even in the unlikely event that not one more cent is dedicated to debt repayment, this measure will continue to fall. Success – in these terms – is guaranteed, it's just a matter of degree. As Finance Minister Manley pointed out in late 2003, "assuming no incremental debt reduction, [the debt-to-GDP ratio] would fall to about 33% by 2008-09. If the Contingency Reserve [worth $3 billion annually] is not needed and is used to reduce federal debt, the federal debt-to-GDP ratio would decline to 31.5% in 2008–09."[34]

But a constant downward trajectory is not sufficiently dramatic for a conquering hero. As Prime Minister and the new leader of the Liberal Party, Paul Martin wants more.

In his only speech in recent months where he spelled out specific elements of his vision for leading the nation, Martin clearly signalled that there would be no fundamental shift in approach from the past decade. In fact, he suggested deepening the revolution, to guarantee its permanency.

> *First, it is absolutely essential that we lower our national debt load, in order to keep our interest rates low, continue to lower taxes, and keep the flexibility we need to respond to an unpredictable international economy. In concrete terms, that means continuing to cut the debt-to-GDP ratio from 71%, where it was in 1997, past 40%, where it is today, back towards the 25% level that Canada had in the late 1960s. Governments must never forget the lessons of prudent fiscal management. That means always keeping a firm grip on spending – especially in the uncertain times now facing the global economy. It means a commitment to an ongoing program review.*

> Paul Martin's Speech to the Board of Trade
> of Metropolitan Montreal, September 18, 2003

There is no economic significance to bringing debt levels to 25% of GDP, but it has plenty of significance historically and politically, especially in the context of the "absolutely essential" need to continue to lower taxes.

The last time federal debt-to-GDP ratios were around 25% was in the 1960s, when federal program spending as a per cent of GDP ranged between 14% and 16%. If the goal was to have the entire scale of government go back to the 1960s, then the feds would be spending at least 2% to

4% of GDP more in programs – between $24 and $48 billion more a year at the current level of GDP.

Returning to the governance style of the 1960s is not the goal, however. The real purpose behind Martin's flagging the 25% mark is to shift the goal-posts of government objectives, precluding significant action on other priorities until that goal is met or redefined.

If the Liberals win the federal election this year and Martin completes a four-year term as Prime Minister, he has served notice that the goal of a debt ratio of 33% or 31% will not be enough for his own definition of success. It will be much lower. A hero does not coast. He wages war. But what are the implications of such a war?

What's next? A Peek at Paul Martin's Leadership Style for Canada

> *We stand together on the edge of historic possibility. At a moment that comes rarely in the life of a country. It is a time when destiny is ours to hold. A time of new opportunity which must be seized upon in a conscious, determined effort... It is a time to turn an historic circumstance into transformative change – to summon a new national will ... We have to build a 21st century economy in Canada for Canadians. We succeeded in the last 10 years because we did not deviate from course – balanced budgets, a continually dropping debt ratio, lower taxes. We must stay that course.*
> Paul Martin's Leadership Convention speech, November 14, 2003

Will Paul Martin the Prime Minister be any different than Paul Martin the Finance Minister? Other than the occasional rhetorical flourish, there is little indication that we will get something fundamentally different than the same old Paul Martin we've seen for the past ten years.

Paul Martin is yesterday's man. He wants the size of government of 1951 (or earlier), the size of the debt from the 1960s. He is looking backwards to offer a future whose trajectory may include a bigger economy, but will guarantee a less integrated and healthy society.

This is indeed a historic moment for the nation. It is a moment that calls not for nation-building, but for nation *re*building.

After more than a decade of deferring the costs of construction and repair of infrastructure that supports businesses and communities across the country, we are faced with two needs: 1) maintain the infrastructure we have, much of which was built half a century ago, in the post-war re-construction era, and is in desperate need of repair; and 2) expand and upgrade infrastructure to meet the needs of a larger, aging population, a more knowledge-intensive economy, and a productive system that must also contend with the clearly emerging limits of taking the environment for granted.

In closing his Budget Speech in 1995, Paul Martin said:

> *Government must begin to plan ahead – not timidly, not tentatively – but boldly, imaginatively and courageously." Those words were spoken by my father in 1957 – for his time. That is what I believe we have done today, for ours.*

Can Paul Martin focus on the future, boldly making the investments that this generation needs? Will his unwavering focus on what came before, in the 1960s, in the 1950s, also eventually acknowledge that the hallmark of that generation was the expansion of public goods, not constraint?

Paul Martin's commitment to continued small government has cast public investments as a drain on capacity, discounting their ability to increase Canada's capacity to grow and prosper more equitably.

Paul Martin's commitment to continued small government has cast public investments as a drain on capacity, discounting their ability to increase Canada's capacity to grow and prosper more equitably, in both economic and social terms. The commitment to small government has emphasized provincial "flexibility" and decentralization for a decade, making new federal initiatives more difficult to launch and poor program take-up mainly an issue of uncooperative provinces. The commitment to small government understands that, shrugs its shoulders, and moves on to aggressive national debt repayment, rather than figuring out what combination of money and politics will prevent our collective foundation and infrastructure from crumbling.

The hallmark of Paul Martin's permanent revolution is the permanent *devolution* of responsibilities: passing the buck (but not the bucks) on to lower levels of government and, ultimately, onto individuals. It implies continued underinvestment in health care, early childhood education, and our cities. It undermines the very nature of the federation. It strangles community capacities and individual opportunities.

The permanent revolution, in the sense which Marx attached to this concept, means a revolution which makes no compromise with any single form of class rule a revolution whose every successive stage is rooted in the preceding one and which can end only in complete liquidation.

Leon Trotsky, first published in St. Petersburg
in 1906, first translated to English in 1921

Paul Martin wants these changes, this revolution, to be permanent. But the sustainability of the small government approach is increasingly in question. Another four years of this agenda could easily move us closer to "complete liquidation," the predicted fruit of permanent revolution according to Trotsky.

Will Paul Martin get away with this agenda in the new political environment without the enabling role of Jean Chrétien? Without doubt, Jean Chrétien's personality humanized the agenda. He kept the show real, rough around the edges, with a hint of humour and a street-fighter's style of leadership we could relate to: muddling through and doing the best you can with the hand you are dealt.

Martin without Chrétien is a new, untested act. Can Canadians warm up to the cold basics of small government without Chrétien to soften the edges? Or will Paul Martin be compelled to shift with the times? In the classic language of the hero, he recently asked us to think forward, to work towards our common destiny.

Together we have the possibility of translating our recent gains into lasting national advantage. I ask all of you to join me in fulfilling Canada's destiny. Now is the time to come together as a country – in common cause and shared determination; united in purpose and accomplishment.

Paul Martin's Speech at the Liberal Leadership
Convention, November 14, 2003

The federal government's coffers and political support are unusually robust at this point in our history. Given this solid foundation, it is entirely possible for a political leader to launch something truly revolutionary for our times: a different kind of social experiment, a quest for a different type of abundance, starting with re-investment in our own future, the future of our children.

Now that would be a permanent revolution worth starting.

Notes

1 Government of Canada, Department of Finance, *Fiscal Reference Tables*, September 2003, Table 55

2 *ibid.*, Table 2. Both 1990 and 2000 were peaks of the business cycle, so the contraction is not due simply to the strengthening of the economy.

3 Government of Canada, *The Budget Plan 2003*, page 213.

4 All figures from Industry Canada, *Departmental Performance Report 2000-2001*, March 31, 2001, Section 2.4. Available on-line at: http://www.ic.gc.ca/cmb/welcomeic.nsf/532340a8523f33718525649d006b119d/030fbd4595e348cd05256b03004eec15!OpenDocument

5 Industry Canada, "2002 in Review," *Monthly Trade Bulletin*, Volume 5, Number 1, March 2003, p.4

6 *ibid.* http://www.ic.gc.ca/cmb/welcomeic.nsf/532340a8523f33718525649d006b119d/012bffa29fcb623885256dc200424073!OpenDocument

7 Industry Canada, Micro-Economic Policy Analysis Branch, *The Trade and Investment Monitor, Fall/Winter 2002,*

8 Industry Canada Performance Report for the period ending March 31, 2003. Section 2.5. http://www.ic.gc.ca/cmb/welcomeic.nsf/532340a8523f33718525649d006b119d/fe1e6b4d199baf1a85256dcf0059e528!OpenDocument

9 Department of Finance Canada, *A Report on Plans and Priorities, 2001-02 Estimates*, p.11 Canada inflation rate is only higher than (deflationary) Japan and France, which has been struggling with deflationary trends in the 1990s.

10 Statistics Canada, *Consumer Price Index*, CANSIM P200000. Note that the Government used the War Measures Act on October 18th, 1941, during World War II, to set limits on wages and prices. The measures were removed in 1945, when the war ended, and prices grew at an annual average of 7% until 1952.

11 http://www.Bank-Banque-Canada.Ca/pdf/annual_page44_page45.pdf, posted Mon, 14 Jan 2002. Real interest rates during the 1940s were slightly lower. Accounting for inflation, which averaged 3.7% over the period, borrowing at the prime rate cost just under 1%. With inflation rates around 2% in early 2002, the real cost of borrowing at the prime rate is just under 2%.

12 Statistics Canada, *National Income and Expenditure Accounts, Quarterly Estimates, Second Quarter 2003*, Catalogue No. 13-001-PPB

[13] Statistics Canada, *The Daily*, June 25, 2003, and October 30, 2002, both entitled Family Income

[14] Statistics Canada, *The Daily*, June 25, 2003, Family Income

[15] Statistics Canada, *The Daily*, July 28, 2000, Income Inequality

[16] "Honouring Our Promises: Meeting the Challenge to End Child and Family Poverty", 2003 *Report Card on Child Poverty in Canada*, Campaign 2000, www.campaign2000.ca. citing the Canadian Housing and Renewal Association, Report to the Parliamentary Standing Committee on Finance. September 23, 2003.

[17] Ontario Non-Profit Housing Association, *Where's Home Update*, released November 16, 2002. http://www.housingagain.web.net/whome/whereshome2001final.pdf

[18] In 1999 the figure was 200,000 according to "Homeless in Canada", News Documentary, CBC-TV, The National, Monday, December 20, 1999. The current figure is supplied by Michael Shapcott, Co-ordinator, Community / University Research Partnerships Unit, Centre for Urban and Community Studies, University of Toronto. For further articles about homelessness visit www.housingagain.web.net.

[19] The Canadian Association of Food Banks, *HungerCount 2003*, p. 3, and Carly Steinman, *A Surplus of Hunger: Canada's Annual Survey of Emergency Food Programs*, prepared for the Canadian Association of Food Banks, October 2000. There are more than 1,300 McDonald's in Canada (Source: McDonald's Canada, www.mcdonalds.ca/en/aboutus/mcdCanada_facts.aspx)

[20] *Something has to give: Food Banks filling the Policy Gap in Canada*, news release, October 16, 2003, Canadian Association of Food Banks, www.cafb-acba.ca.

[21] "[Premier] Harris accepts the blame", *The Globe and Mail*, January 19, 2002, page A1

[22] *Tuition Fees in Canada: A Pan-Canadian Perspective on Educational User Fees*, Canadian Federation of Students, September 2001, Vol 7., No. 5, www.cfs-fcee.ca

[23] Statistics Canada, *Census 2001*, Catalogue 97F0019XCB01041

[24] OECD, *Health at a Glance – OECD Indicators*, October 16, 2003. http://www.oecd.org/dataoecd/20/2/16494895.pdf

[25] Globe and Mail, *Canada's MD shortage among worst in Western world*, October 16, 2003

[26] Statistics Canada, *The Daily*, July 15, 2002, Health Services Access Survey 2001

27 Armine Yalnizyan, *What Would They Do with The Surplus?* Ottawa: Canadian Centre for Policy Alternatives, November 2000, pp. iv and 6.

28 *Annual Financial Report of the Government of Canada, Fiscal Year 2002-3*, Page 9, Table 1

29 The capital tax reductions will cost $455 million by 2004-05, but there is no indication what the full elimination of this tax would mean. Federal capital taxes will be eliminated by 2008. Increasing the RRSP/RPP limits to $15,000 from $13,500 will cost a further $295 million until 2004-5.

30 *The Budget Plan 2003*, Table A1.2, page 229.

31 Government of Canada, Department of Finance, *Fiscal Reference Tables October 2003, Tables 2 and 57.*

32 Government of Canada, Department of Finance, *Annual Financial Report, Fiscal Year 2002- 2003, page 7.*

33 *The Budget Plan 2003*, p. 216.

34 Department of Finance, *Economic and Fiscal Update 2003 Private Sector Five-Year Economic and Fiscal Projections*, October 29, 2003, page 97.

CHAPTER 2

Paul Martin, the Deficit,
and the Debt
Taking Another Look

by Jim Stanford

B alancing the federal budget is Paul Martin's greatest claim to fame.
As Finance Minister of the newly-elected Liberal government, he inherited a dismal fiscal situation – with a deficit equal to 6% of GDP (large by
any measure, though still smaller than the 8% deficits Ottawa incurred in
the early 1980s), and a burden of accumulated debt whose growth (net
federal debt had doubled in the previous ten years as a share of Canada's
GDP) was obviously unsustainable. Martin's first budget, in 1994, was
mostly a "stand-pat" exercise, as the new Finance Minister grappled with
the dimensions of the problem and considered different options for addressing it. But his second budget, delivered on February 27, 1995, became a watershed moment in Canada's economic and social history. For
with that budget, Martin indicated, first, that the deficit would be defeated – as he famously put it, "come hell or high water." More importantly, he revealed *how* it would be defeated: mostly through an unprecedented frontal attack on federal programs, through which Ottawa's non-
military spending (on everything from unemployment benefits to provincial transfer payments to foreign aid) was cut back more dramatically than
at any time in our national history.[1]

The rest of the story is well known. Martin's attack on the deficit won him immediate, enthusiastic plaudits from the business and financial communities – all the more so because they understood that the change in Ottawa's fiscal stance was considerably more aggressive than Martin's official numbers seemed to indicate. At first, Canada's macroeconomy stalled for some time in the face of deep public spending cutbacks (real GDP actually contracted briefly late in 1995). But then, helped along by low interest rates and exports to the booming U.S. economy, growth picked up quickly. Powered by the combination of declining spending, falling interest costs, and ballooning tax revenues, the federal deficit disappeared suddenly, almost miraculously. By fiscal 1997 – just two years after Martin had steeled the nation for a long and painful battle, and two full years ahead of his own official timetable – Ottawa was back in the black for the first time in a generation, ahead of any other G-7 economy.

Martin's second budget, delivered on February 27, 1995, became a watershed moment in Canada's economic and social history. The deficit would be defeated – as he famously put it, "come hell or high water."

With this quicker-than-expected victory over the deficit, Martin's reputation as a prudent, no-nonsense, business-friendly administrator was cemented. He became the brightest, most important star in the Chrétien cabinet, eventually eclipsing the Prime Minister himself. Of course, Martin remained Finance Minister for several years after his defining triumph; it's harder to pin down a sense of his major subsequent accomplishments. He oversaw the creation of several "endowed" federal foundations, funded from the convenient year-end surpluses that seemed to magically appear in Ottawa after 1997, to support favoured Liberal projects like innovation and university scholarships. He headed up negotiations with the provinces to repair some of the damage done by the earlier cuts in federal transfers, culminating in the pre-election health accord signed late in 2000. But none of these projects or priorities compares with the credibility and popularity he won as a result of eliminating the deficit. If Paul Martin had retired in 2002 (rather than being exiled to the Liberal back-benches), he would be remembered first and foremost as the man who balanced Ottawa's budget. And depending, of course, on his experience as Prime Minister, that may still prove to be his defining achievement.

There is no doubt that Canada faced a serious fiscal situation when the Liberals were elected in 1993. There is no disagreement that the deficit had to be dramatically reduced or eliminated, and, more importantly, that the upward track in the federal debt burden had to be quickly arrested and reversed. And there is no doubt that, by these indicators, Canada has been a fiscal star among the group of industrialized countries since Paul Martin became Finance Minister. But it may well be that Martin's stellar reputation as a tough and prudent budgeter is not fully deserved. A broader second look at Canada's finances during the Martin era suggests that important errors may have been made on the road to the balanced budget, producing unnecessary but lasting social and economic harm.

The deficit was eliminated more quickly, and with a much greater emphasis on program spending cuts, than was the case in virtually any other industrialized country (18 of which, in total, balanced their budgets during approximately the same time frame as Canada). When Canadians express concern today about the quality and safety of public services and infrastructure – like health care, education, and water – they might well reconsider the wisdom of Martin's deliberate choice to attack the deficit in the particular way that he did. At the same time, some of the budgetary practices which Martin established as Finance Minister, justified initially by the need for Ottawa to rebuild credibility with financial analysts and lenders, have subsequently imparted a consistently misleading and manipulative tendency to federal budgeting.

In sum, then, Martin's fiscal legacy is more complex than simply that he "balanced the budget." His legacy includes a budget that was balanced more quickly, and more violently, than it needed to be. And it also includes a highly politicized culture of budget-making that is no more reliable or transparent than the "rose-coloured" budgets of earlier years that Martin himself so successfully critiqued.

Eliminating the Deficit

Canada was the first G-7 economy to balance its budget in the late 1990s, as governments across the OECD collectively recovered from the fiscal damage done by the global recession and high interest rates of the early 1990s. Considering that Canada started out with relatively large deficits, our early attainment of a balanced budget is certainly noteworthy. As indicated in Figure 1, Canada's total public deficits (federal and provincial) from 1991 through 1993 averaged 8% of GDP – twice the OECD average.[2] Only Italy had a larger deficit at that time among the G-7 economies, and only Italy carried a larger burden of accumulated debt. It could certainly be argued in 1994 that Canada required relatively strong deficit-fighting medicine, to overcome a relatively weak fiscal position and catch up with the rest of the industrialized world.

In fact, of course, something rather different occurred. Canada not only caught up with other G-7 countries, it quickly surpassed them in the speed of deficit reduction. Already by 1996, Canada's deficit was smaller than any other G-7 economy but the U.S., and by the next year the deficit was history (beating other G-7 economies to a balanced budget by one to three years). Clearly, Canada's approach to deficit reduction was relatively and deliberately aggressive. In retrospect, it is difficult to argue that we had "no choice" but to eliminate the deficit as quickly as we did, when other industrialized countries – including those with even larger deficits and debts – accomplished the task much more gradually.

At the same time, Figure 1 also indicates that the return to fiscal balance during the late 1990s was experienced relatively broadly across the OECD. Fiscal balances in almost all industrialized countries improved notably through the latter 1990s, as indicated by the broad fiscal pattern

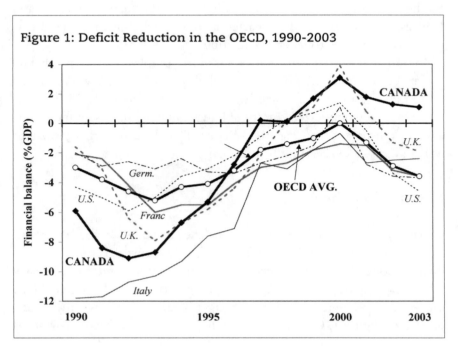

Figure 1: Deficit Reduction in the OECD, 1990-2003

portrayed in Figure 1.[3] So Canada's fiscal guardians cannot claim any particular triumph in overseeing the turnaround in public finances, nor in achieving the milestone of a balanced budget. Indeed, a total of 18 OECD countries balanced their budgets late in the decade (and most of the others came within spitting distance of doing so). The primary drivers of this broad-based improvement in fiscal performance were the acceleration in global growth and a steep decline in global interest rates (which spurred growth and had the added benefit of reducing governments' own debt servicing expenses).[4] The "tough choices" and "prudent planning" so emphasized by Finance Canada officials as being the root source of Canada's fiscal progress might explain why Canada improved its finances more aggressively than other countries; but clearly, most of that improvement would have occurred anyway, as a result of the same favourable factors which explain the widespread fiscal recovery experienced in most other countries at the same time.

There is one aspect of Canada's fiscal turnaround, however, that is truly unique in the international comparison. As indicated in Figure 2, Canadian governments implemented much deeper reductions in government program spending than any other major industrialized country – including those (like Italy) which faced even more severe fiscal problems. Gen-

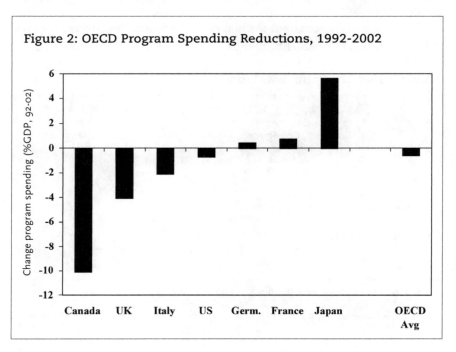

Figure 2: OECD Program Spending Reductions, 1992-2002

eral government program spending, measured as a share of GDP, declined by 10 percentage points in Canada between 1992 and 2002. In the OECD as a whole, over the same period, program spending stayed roughly constant as a share of GDP. So, while most OECD countries balanced their budgets during the late 1990s, this goal was not attained in other countries by slashing and burning government programs. Indeed, countries like the U.S., Germany, and France restored fiscal balance with hardly any spending cuts at all – and in some cases, while actually *increasing* government spending.

For the federal government, these program spending cutbacks accounted for the lion's share of the burden of deficit-reduction. As summarized in Table 1, from 1993 (the final budget before the Liberals came to power) through 1997 (when the budget was balanced), the federal budget balance improved by a total of 5.3 percentage points of GDP. Reductions in federal program spending (similarly measured as a share of GDP) accounted for two-thirds of this progress. Tax increases accounted for 22% of the reduction in the deficit (although they garnered a disproportionate share of the attention in the headlines of certain business-oriented newspapers). A small decline in the relative importance of debt service charges (thanks to lower interest rates) contributed the remaining progress toward eliminating the deficit.

There was no choice about the federal government's need to reduce the deficit in the early 1990s. But there *were* clear choices about how to do it.

Table 1: How the Battle Was Won			
	1993 to 1997		1997 to 2002
	Change as % GDP	Share of Total "Sacrifice"[1]	Change as % GDP
Revenues	+1.2%	22%	-1.8%
Program Spending	-3.6%	67%	-0.6%
Debt Service Charges	-0.6%	11%	-1.7%
Total Budget Balance	+5.3%	100%	+0.4%

Source: Author's calculations from Department of Finance, *Fiscal Reference Tables* (full accrual accounting).

1. Change in budget category (as share of GDP) as proportion total improvement in budget balance (as share of GDP).

Under Paul Martin's leadership, Ottawa focused its guns mostly on reducing program spending – with social and economic consequences that are still being felt today. Those spending cuts were far deeper than experienced in other industrialized economies. Italy, for example, demonstrated a roughly equal degree of fiscal progress as Canada (reducing its deficit, relative to GDP, by a similar amount from trough to peak); yet program spending cutbacks in Italy were one-fifth as large as in Canada. In most other OECD countries, program spending remained stable or even increased relative to GDP. *The fact that Canada's public sector programs were cut back so dramatically was not the inevitable result of a fiscal crisis. It reflected, rather, the deliberate choices of our government.* Today, Canadians express a great deal of concern about the state of essential public services and infrastructure, like health care, education, and public transportation. This concern suggests that Martin's failure to protect those assets and programs, even though a clear fiscal opportunity existed to do (while still accepting the need to reduce or eliminate the deficit), was a major policy failure – not the triumph it is usually portrayed as.

It is important to note that, since Ottawa balanced its budget, the emphasis on program spending has been replaced with an emphasis on tax cuts. From 1997 through 2002, tax revenues declined by almost 2 points of GDP (ending up notably lower than when the Liberals came to office). Incredibly, however, program spending has continued to decline relative to GDP since the budget was balanced. Meanwhile, debt service charges have also begun to decline rapidly relative to GDP (in line with the shrinking debt burden, as a share of GDP). The government has enjoyed ample fiscal room since 1997 to restore resources for the public programs and services which bore the brunt of earlier deficit-reduction. The fact that it has not notably done so provides additional proof that its earlier spending cuts were indeed a deliberate choice – not a fiscal necessity.

If balancing the budget were the only goal of government, it could achieve this balance simply by closing down its operations completely, ceasing both tax collections and expenditures. Obviously, the more chal-

> Today, Canadians express a great deal of concern about the state of essential public services and infrastructure. This concern suggests that Martin's failure to protect those assets and programs was a major policy failure – not the triumph it is usually portrayed as.

lenging task is to balance the budget in a manner that allows government to also meet its broader responsibility to enhance the well-being and security of its citizens. There is no doubt that the federal government in the 1990s, under the leadership of Finance Minister Paul Martin, balanced its budget quickly, and that this represented a sharp turnaround from its recent history of chronic deficits and accumulating debt. But Martin's decisions to eliminate the deficit extraordinarily quickly, and mostly on the basis of painful spending cuts which were not fiscally necessary, are more dubious. Many other countries balanced their budgets, almost as quickly as Canada, but with a fraction of the damage to public programs and infrastructure. As Canadians spend more time waiting for hospital treatment and boiling their tap water, they might well begin to question whether our experience with deficit-elimination was really as successful as it is typically described.

The Debt Burden

The turnaround in Canada's public indebtedness since the mid-1990s has been, if anything, even more dramatic than the elimination of the deficit. In the early 1990s, newspaper headlines warned that Canada would soon hit the "debt wall." These reports were grossly exaggerated, but there is no doubt that Canada's accumulated public debt was growing at an unsustainable pace. The federal government turned the debt corner in 1995 – coincident with Paul Martin's "hell or high water" budget – as the debt (while still growing in nominal terms) was stabilized as a share of GDP. Once the deficit was eliminated, of course, then the decline in the debt burden was accelerated. As indicated in Figure 3, the net federal debt (including "in-house" or non-market debt, such as public service pension obligations) has declined from over 70% of GDP at peak to less than 45% in just seven years.

As with the deficit, Canada went from being a laggard among its industrialized peers to a leader, in a very short space of time. In 1995, when Paul Martin tabled his famous budget, Canada's net federal debt was the second-highest in the G-7 (next to Italy). By 2002, it was the second-lowest, behind only the U.K. – and we will surpass the U.K. within the next couple of years if present trends continue.

It seems incredible, in retrospect, that public indebtedness, which anti-debt crusaders liked to describe in epochal, historic terms ("saddling our children and grandchildren with debt for generations") could so quickly evaporate. Most of the "work" in this impressive debt reduction was carried by the expansion of Canada's GDP. The size of the economy determines a country's ability to service a debt; it is the denominator of the debt/GDP ratio (the most important indicator of the intensity of public indebtedness). The federal debt burden fell by 26 points of GDP between 1995 and 2002, from 70.9% to 44.2%. Five-sixths of that decline was due to the expansion of GDP. One-sixth was due to the repayment of nominal debt, which declined by $50 billion during this time as a result of six consecutive federal surpluses. In other words, if Ottawa had simply balanced its books since 1997, instead of repaying $50 billion worth of debt, the federal debt ratio at the end of 2002 would have equalled 48.8% of GDP, instead of 44.2%. That would still have qualified us as having the second-lowest debt ratio in the G-7.

This result casts incredible doubt on the wisdom of the federal government's decision to allocate billions of dollars worth of the so-called "fiscal dividend" (the fiscal room resulting from the elimination of the deficit and the decline in interest costs) to discretionary debt repayment. In terms of the broad state of public indebtedness, that $50 billion in debt repayment (much of it attained by "stealth" thanks to deliberately conservative

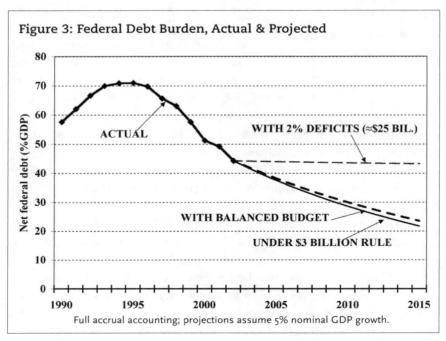

Figure 3: Federal Debt Burden, Actual & Projected

Full accrual accounting; projections assume 5% nominal GDP growth.

budgeting assumptions designed to create "surprising" year-end surpluses) has made virtually no visible difference. *Our debt burden is hardly any lower than it would have been if the federal government had simply balanced its books. On the other hand, that $50 billion would have made an incredible difference to the concrete quality of Canadians' lives if it had been invested in repairing some of the damage that was done to public programs and infrastructure earlier in the 1990s.*

In the period since the budget was balanced, Canadians have grappled with drinking water that can kill them, medical waiting times that impose incalculable stress on patients and their families, and schools driven to sign contracts with soft-drink companies in order to buy textbooks. Meanwhile, their federal government was allocating $50 billion in scarce resources to ensure that our debt burden equalled 44.2% of GDP rather than 48.8%. Was this "prudent" fiscal management? Millions of Canadians probably beg to differ.

> Our debt burden is hardly any lower than it would have been if the federal government had simply balanced its books. On the other hand, that $50 billion would have made an incredible difference to the concrete quality of Canadians' lives.

What is typically described in the financial pages as a prudent act, setting aside tens of billions of dollars of scarce resources for extra incremental reductions in a debt burden that is already shrinking rapidly, could be seen as recklessly *im*prudent if we consider the pressing alternative uses to which those resources should have been dedicated. For example, any homeowner who ignored obvious signs that his or her house foundation was crumbling in order to make discretionary extra mortgage payments would not generally be considered "prudent;" they would be considered incredibly misguided for neglecting the maintenance of their primary asset. Ignore the foundation, and the house falls down. The homeowner is then left with a smaller mortgage, but a pile of rubble.

Going forward, the federal government will face similar choices regarding the wisdom of discretionary repayment of its nominal debt. Martin indicated before his elevation to Prime Minister, in a speech to the Montreal Board of Trade, that he preferred to see the debt burden continue to shrink until it reached 25% of GDP. As indicated in Figure 3, this will occur by 2012 if the government continues its official practice of allocating $3 billion annually to debt repayment (in practice, of course,

Ottawa has allocated much more than this to debt repayment, in which case the 25% goal would be achieved sooner).[5] If the government simply balanced its budget (rather than setting aside $3 billion annually for debt repayment), the 25% goal would be reached in 2013 – a whole year later. This demonstrates once again the economic irrelevance of the official $3 billion debt repayment plan. It will not produce any significant difference in a trajectory of indebtedness that is driven fundamentally by the fact that the nominal debt is not growing (with the budget balanced) while the economy is. Again, Canadians should consider carefully whether or not these $3 billion annual repayments are genuinely "prudent." Which would they consider to be the more important, and prudent, act of government: say, a national public housing program which could help to eliminate homelessness (a generous federal contribution to which would be $3 billion per year), or making sure that our debt/GDP ratio declines to 25% by 2012 instead of 2013?

It is interesting to note that, if the federal government wanted to simply *stabilize* its debt/GDP profile (rather than seeing the debt burden continue to shrink) in the context of continuing economic growth,[6] it would *need* to incur modest annual deficits. As indicated in Figure 3, Ottawa could incur deficits equivalent to 2% of GDP (currently equal to almost $25 billion per year) without increasing its real debt burden. Ottawa's current indebtedness is now low, by both historic and international standards, and its ability to comfortably service that debt is not in question. The government could, if it chose, incur relatively small annual deficits without boosting its debt ratio at all.[7] Several important OECD economies, like Germany and France, have followed something like this strategy. Instead of making a fetish out of constantly reducing nominal debt, they have pursued a more moderate position that recognizes the need for long-term stability in the debt ratio but tolerates modest deficits when required (due either to macroeconomic conditions or pressing social priorities). In Canada, however, this discussion is a purely academic one because of the political culture that is the legacy of our 1990s infatuation with eliminating the deficit. No government, at either the provincial or the federal level, would now dare to countenance a fiscal plan which allowed for regular, modest deficits – even though such an approach is clearly feasible in economic terms.

Eventually, however, the day will come when government may indeed want to consider just such an option. Martin has in essence indicated that present federal practices – annual modest debt repayment – should continue for roughly another decade. But what then? Should the debt ratio continue to fall until it reaches zero – and, indeed, should government then carry on piling up surpluses (in the form of accumulated net assets which might be invested, for example, in corporate equities, as is the practice in some Scandinavian countries)? If not, then Martin will eventually need to countenance small regular deficits in order to stabilize the debt at his desired level. If the federal government under Martin continues its recent practice of allocating much more than $3 billion per year to debt repayment, then this decision point will come sooner – perhaps as early as the end of Martin's first mandate.

Many observers have praised Paul Martin for his "business-like approach" to managing public finances. Yet the notion that a debt burden should be reduced continually, as a matter of planning priority, in the context of a demonstrated ability to comfortably service that debt, is anathema in business circles. Businesses, like governments, must maintain their indebtedness at serviceable levels. But no real-world CEO would suggest that a moderate and serviceable debt load should be continually reduced as a matter of corporate priority. If there was no better use for the company's free cash flow (due to an absence of adequately profitable investment opportunities), then it might consider extra debt repayment as a default. Investors and shareholders, however, would look dubiously upon any business which passed up good investment opportunities because of an infatuation with reducing debt from a moderate level to a near-zero level. Yet this is exactly the strategy upon which the federal government is currently embarked. Important opportunities to invest in Canada and Canadians are being passed over so that Canada can reduce its debt from a moderate level to an ultra-low level. The "shareholders" of this enterprise should start asking some tough questions of its "senior management."

Never Again?

The issue of whether or not the federal debt burden should be continually reduced is related to the issue of whether the federal government should ever tolerate another deficit. When debt levels are high (as in the early 1990s), then it is clear that they should be reduced. That implies the elimination of deficits, followed by a period of sustained debt reduction (driven mostly by ongoing economic growth).[8] At more moderate levels, however, it is not clear why government would make the avoidance of a deficit an overarching economic and political priority. With a debt burden equal to 40% of GDP, as indicated in Figure 3, Ottawa could experience annual modest deficits with no damage to its debt rating; alternatively, it could incur more substantial deficits for shorter periods of time, so long as it was clear that those deficits were temporary (rather than structural) in nature. Yet Paul Martin, along with many of his provincial counterparts, has made solemn promises that his government will never again slip back into the red. In some provinces, this near-religious approach to deficit-prevention has been enshrined in "balanced budget laws" and other, mostly symbolic legislation to purportedly "prevent" future governments from running deficits.[9]

At the provincial level, the recent return of large deficits (the result in part of the painful fiscal downloading which Martin engineered in order to solve his own deficit problem) indicates that deficit-avoidance can be readily overruled by other public concerns (like demands for more health care and education spending, for instance). At the federal level, too, it is easy to imagine a situation in which the government – driven either by an economic downturn, or by urgent social or public health and safety issues – might want to once again incur a deficit. So long as federal deficits do not become both large and chronic, they can clearly be tolerated on economic grounds. But the fact that Martin has attempted to make them intolerable, on political grounds, unduly limits the flexibility of the federal government for dealing with such circumstances in the future.

Since Martin's defining political achievement was the elimination of the federal deficit, it is not surprising that he should want to emphasize that his government will never, under any circumstance, return to a deficit position. But this is an economically and politically imprudent position to adopt.

Since Martin's defining political achievement was the elimination of the federal deficit, it is not surprising that he should want to emphasize that his government will never, under any circumstance, return to a deficit position.[10] But this is an economically and politically imprudent position to adopt. Given the sea change in the federal debt profile since 1995, Ottawa could clearly incur large deficits for a short period of time, or small deficits on an ongoing basis, with no damage to the economic and financial health of the country. That Martin has ruled out such a possibility, and has made deficit-avoidance an inviolable priority of his government (more important than addressing some future public health emergency, for example?), may yet prove to be a painful and costly error.

Was There Any Choice?

The preceding discussion has hinted that the federal government, under the leadership of Finance Minister Martin, had significantly more room to manoeuvre during the difficult fiscal situation of the mid-1990s than the government and Martin admitted. It eliminated the deficit in a more aggressive fashion than occurred in other countries, and utilized a uniquely focused attack on government program spending. The government ended up beating its own deficit-reduction timetable by two years, and was similarly ahead of other industrialized countries in the race to the balanced budget. Initially, Canadians were relieved that the fiscal situation had turned around so markedly. More recently, however, they have expressed deep concern over the state of essential public services (especially health care). Of course, these two sets of issues – relief over the sea change in federal finances, but concern over essential public services – are linked. Can we look back to consider more explicitly what would have happened if the federal government, under Martin, had adopted a more gradual and balanced approach to deficit reduction?

In reality, of course, Martin's spending cuts were far more aggressive than were required by his own timetable

Table 2 summarizes the results of a counterfactual simulation to consider how the deficit could have been eliminated without any nominal program spending cuts whatsoever, according to exactly the same *official* timetable laid out by Martin in his famous 1995 budget.[11] At that time, Martin promised to reduce the deficit to no more than 3% of GDP during fiscal 1996, 2% by fiscal 1997, and 1% in 1998 (leading, presumably, to a balanced budget by fiscal 1999). In reality, of course, Martin's spending cuts were far more aggressive than were required by his own timetable (a fact which business and financial commentators understood well, thus amplifying their praise for his budget). Table 2 summarizes two deficit reduction scenarios: the actual experience of the federal government from 1994 through 1999 (top portion), and a counterfactual scenario which assumes the federal government only *froze* nominal program spending at its 1994 levels (rather than implementing the deep spending cuts that began with the 1995 budget). The counterfactual scenario also assumes that Canada's nominal GDP growth during 1995 and 1996 (the period of nominal spending cutbacks) would have been strengthened by the amount of the spending cutback.[12] On the basis of other plausible assumptions regarding average effective tax rates and average effective interest rates (which are assumed constant in the two scenarios), the federal government would still have beaten its official deficit reduction timetable and balanced the budget by fiscal 1999[13] *with no cuts in nominal program spending, and no*

Table 2: Actual and Simulated Deficit Reduction, 1994-1999

	1994	1995	1996	1997	1998	1999
Official deficit target (%GDP)			-3.0	-2.0	-1.0	0.0
Actual Experience						
Nominal GDP growth(%)		5.6	3.1	4.3	3.2	7.6
Revenue ($b)	123.3	130.3	140.9	153.2	155.7	160.0
Program spending ($b)	118.7	112	104.8	108.8	111.4	115.5
Debt service ($b)	42.0	46.9	45.0	40.9	41.4	41.5
Balance (%GDP)	-4.8	-3.5	-1.1	0.4	0.3	0.3
Counterfactual Simulation: Frozen Nominal Program Spending						
Nominal GDP growth(%)		6.5	4.0	4.3	3.2	7.6
Revenue ($b)	123.3	131.4	143.3	155.8	158.3	162.7
Program spending ($b)	118.7	118.7	118.7	118.7	118.7	118.7
Debt service ($b)	42.0	47.1	45.9	42.5	43.6	44.1
Balance (%GDP)	-4.8	-4.2	-2.5	-0.6	-0.4	0.0

Counterfactual simulation assumes identical revenue/GDP ratio and average effective interest rate as in actual experience; program spending is frozen at 1994 nominal level; GDP growth adjusted by the amount of the foregone program spending cutbacks in 1995 and 1996; and debt accumulation and debt service charges adjusted accordingly.

additional increases in aggregate taxation (other than those which were in fact imposed by the federal government).

In this context, the claim that the only alternatives to deep program spending cuts would have been either the continuing indefinite accumulation of public debt, or else the imposition of dramatic tax increases, is not credible. Paul Martin could have overseen the quick elimination of the huge deficit which his government inherited, in line with his own timetable, *yet without imposing a single dollar of nominal program spending reductions.*[14] The fact that so many other industrialized countries also eliminated deficits during the latter 1990s, most of them more gradually than Canada, and most without dramatic reductions in program expenditure, similarly supports the notion that real choices were available, while still accepting the general goal of deficit reduction. So Martin's decision to impose dramatic program spending reductions to attain a uniquely fast improvement in bottom-line fiscal balances must, therefore, have reflected priorities other than simply the desire to balance the budget. Instead of concluding that Martin is a hero for leading Canadians in an epic battle to eliminate the deficit (a battle which, after all, 18 OECD countries in total accomplished), perhaps we should be asking why he implemented such dramatic reductions in government programs that have been enduringly painful, yet, in retrospect, were unnecessary. Our new Prime Minister might then be wreathed in a different aura indeed.

Honesty and Transparency in Budgeting

One additional feature of Martin's fiscal legacy has been the adoption of a set of budget-making practices and procedures designed to insulate the budget from negative fiscal shocks, but also to insulate the government from demands for additional spending. Beginning with his famous 1995 budget, Martin invented the practice of including an explicit "contingency fund" within the budget (initially set at $2.5 billion, and subsequently increased to $3 billion). The purpose of this fund was to provide a financial cushion against negative fiscal developments during the upcoming year (such as economic downturn or unforeseen emergency expenditures), allowing the government to still meet its bottom-line target. Under Martin's leadership, other conservative planning practices also became standard features of federal budget-making. For example, on top of the contingency reserve, some budgets and forecasts also set aside additional resources for "economic prudence," to provide fiscal protection against negative economic events. The macroeconomic forecasts used to project government revenues were usually adjusted relative to average private-sector forecasts (by reducing assumed growth rates, and increasing assumed interest rates) to similarly build fiscal wiggle-room into the budgets. Internally, it also appears that the government's estimates (of incoming revenues, and outgoing expenses – especially for debt service charges) were further padded. For example, even after allowing for deliberately conservative economic growth assumptions, revenue forecasts in most of Martin's budgets were too low, reflecting additional behind-the-scenes efforts to paint a deliberately bleak picture of Ottawa's finances.

The predictable result of these practices has been a pattern of consistent but increasingly phony fiscal "overperformance." Since Martin's first budget in 1994, Ottawa has beaten its own bottom-line budget targets nine years in a row (see Figure 4). The cumulative "overperformance" (actual balance versus budgeted balance) now equals a staggering $80 billion. In fiscal 1997, the government beat its budget target by an incredible $20 billion – missing the mark by a greater margin than any other budget in Canadian history. In 1996 and again in 2000, the year-end results came in $15 billion above target. On average over these nine years, Ottawa beat its own official targets by just under $9 billion per year.

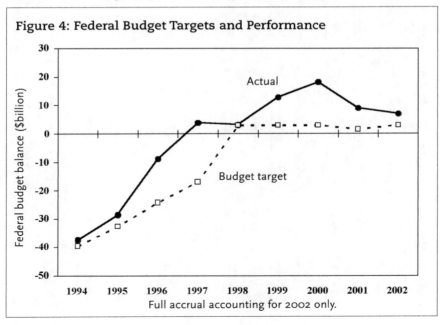

Figure 4: Federal Budget Targets and Performance

Full accrual accounting for 2002 only.

Table 3   Hit and Miss: Liberal Budgeting Errors by Category

	Revenues			Program Spending			Debt Service			Budget Balance		
	Budget	Actual	%Error	Budget	Actual	%Error	Budget	Actual	%Error	Budget	Actual	$bError
1994/95	123.9	123.3	-0.5	122.6	118.7	-3.2%	41.0	42.0	+2.4%	-39.7	-37.5	+2.2
1995/96	133.2	130.3	-2.2	114.0	112.0	-1.8%	49.5	46.9	-5.3%	-32.7	-28.6	+4.1
1996/97	135.0	140.9	+4.4%	109.0	104.8	-3.9%	47.8	45.0	-5.9%	-24.3	-8.9	+15.4
1997/98	137.8	153.5	+11.4%	105.8	108.8	+2.8%	46.0	40.9	-11.1%	-17.0	3.8	+20.8
1998/99	151.0	155.9	+3.2%	104.5	111.4	+6.6%	43.5	41.4	-4.8%	3.0²	3.1	+0.1
1999/2000	156.7	166.1	+6.0%	111.2	111.8	+0.5%	42.5	41.6	-2.1%	3.0	12.7	+9.7
2000/01	162.0	179.6	+10.9%	116.0	119.3	+2.8%	42.0	42.1	+0.2%	3.0	18.1	+15.1
2001/02	171.3	173.3	+1.2%	130.5	126.7	-2.9%	39.2	37.7	-3.8%	1.5	8.9	+7.4
2002/03¹	173.9	177.6	+2.1%	134.3	133.3	-0.7%	35.6	37.3	+4.8%	3.0	7.0	+4.0
Average			+4.1%			+0.0%			-2.8%			+$8.8 b

Source: Author's calculations from annual Budget Plans. Full accrual accounting for 2002/03 only.

1. No formal budget was delivered for 2002/03; budgeted items are as reported in 2002 *Economic and Fiscal Update*.

2. Beginning in 1998, the government pledged to use its contingency fund (equal to $3 billion in most years) for debt repayment if not needed to cover budgetary shortfalls; this table assumes that the contingency fund is thus the targeted balance (rather than the officially stated zero balance). If the official budget balance target were utilized (instead of the contingency fund) as the target, then the average error over the 9 budgets would have equalled $10.3 billion.

Initially, Finance Ministers professed pleasant surprise at these "upside" errors, attributing them to a combination of favourable economic circumstances and "prudent" fiscal management. It soon became clear, however, that there was nothing accidental about this overperformance: it was pre-ordained by a set of artificial assumptions and practices, all oriented toward making Ottawa's fiscal situation look worse than it actually was. In the dark days of Martin's first budgets, this promoted a politically convenient national ethos that the situation was grim, and belt-tightening was inevitable. Once the deficit was eliminated, replaced by large surpluses, these funny accounting techniques helped to deflect increasingly urgent public demands for investments in health care, education, and infrastructure. After nine straight years, however, the practice has created a situation in which nobody believes the numbers that the Finance Minister of the day tables in his or her official budget. The budget has ceased to be a document in which the government describes its planned operations and seeks Parliamentary approval for them. Rather, the budget has now become a singularly political document, with the primary goal of managing (or manipulating) public expectations.

> Initially, Finance Ministers professed pleasant surprise at these "upside" errors, attributing them to a combination of favourable economic circumstances and "prudent" fiscal management.

Table 3 provides a breakdown of the sources for the Liberal government's consistent budgeting errors. Underestimating its revenues is the major source of the government's financial cushioning. In most years since 1994, Ottawa's budgets have underestimated true revenues by an average during this time of over 4% (worth $7 billion of revenues, given today's tax take by Ottawa). This consistent underestimation reflects the explicit adoption of deliberately conservative economic growth assumptions, as well as additional efforts behind the scenes to underestimate revenues (even in light of those conservative economic assumptions). The budgets have been much closer to the mark, however, in projections of program spending. On average, over the nine Liberal budgets, actual program spending has hit budgeted levels almost exactly (exceeding budgeted levels by just two-hundreths of a percent, on average, during this period).[15] Surprisingly, the official budgets also have a very poor record in forecasting debt service charges, which should be one of the most stable and predictable

budget categories.[16] On average over the nine budgets, Ottawa overestimated its actual debt service charges by 3% (or about $1.2 billion per
year).

The combined result of all this "padding" (both explicit and implicit) is
a budget balance that is almost guaranteed to exceed expectations. Table 4
indicates that the true, total "prudence" factor contained in federal budgets since Martin became Finance Minister has contributed an average of
over $10 billion per year in fiscal wiggle-room to each budget. Only a
portion of this – the $3 billion contingency fund – is explicitly recognized
by the Finance Minister. The rest is hidden behind the scenes in conservative and misleading assumptions and forecasts. No wonder the federal government has so handily beaten its own budget targets, year after
year. It would have been impossible for it not to, given the fiscal cushioning which is now a standard feature of each budget.

There is a very powerful theorem in economics – the "rational expectations" theorem – which holds that economic agents, if they are systematically wrong in their forecasts and judgments, will adjust their forecasting
assumptions so as to be closer to the mark. The experience of federal
budget-making under Paul Martin and his successor, however, would seem

Table 4: Total "Prudence" in Federal Budgets, 1994 through 2002	
Source of "Prudence"	Amount ($billion)
Contingency Reserve Fund	3.0
Additional Economic "Prudence"[1]	0.0 – 3.0
Underestimation of Revenues	
• Conservative economic assumptions	
• Underestimation of revenues in light of those assumptions	7.0[2]
Overestimation of Interest Costs	1.0[3]
Total Average Financial Cushion (per year)	11.0 – 14.0

Source: Author's calculations as described in notes to Table 3.

1. The economic "prudence" cushion is usually applied in longer-run fiscal projections associated with
   the annual Economic and Fiscal Update, although it has on occasion been applied to the two-year
   projections contained in the annual Budget Plan.
2. On average, revenues were underestimated during the nine fiscal years from 1994 through 2002 by
   over 4 percent, equal to $7 billion at current taxation levels.
3. On average, interest costs were overestimated during the nine fiscal years from 1994 through 2002
   by almost 3 percent, equal to over $1 billion at current levels.

to disprove this theorem. In fact, of course, the official budget targets contained in the budget each year should not be confused with what the government actually believes will unfold. Those targets are the product of a deliberately manipulative budget-making process that was initially intended to "restore confidence" in Ottawa's ability to meet its fiscal commitments, but has since contributed to a lamentable politicization of the entire budget-making process.

Instead of facilitating an honest debate among Canadians about how available resources should most effectively be allocated, and to what priorities, Finance officials expend more energy trying to convince Canadians that those resources are not even there. As a result, the only thing we now know for sure about official budget forecasts is that they are not intended to be accurate. And the inevitable year-end fiscal surpluses which are the obvious result of this practice end up usurping (to the delight of the financial community) resources which Canadians quite likely would have preferred to be directed elsewhere. This aspect of federal budget-making is perhaps Paul Martin's most dubious legacy as Finance Minister.

Martin and his supporters will claim that deliberate caution in budgeting was necessary in light of the tendency by past governments to fall well below their budget targets. Back in 1995, when Canada faced a serious debt problem, perhaps this argument was justified. Today, however, there is nothing "prudent" about budgets which are consistently, and deliberately, billions of dollars off of their underlying true values. In the private sector, this type of budgeting would not be tolerated. Even if the financial "surprises" were consistently on the "upside" (as has been the case with Ottawa since 1994), analysts and investors alike would quickly demand more accurate and transparent information, so that they could make their choices and adjust their portfolios in line with reality (rather than a politically convenient fiction). Our federal government, however, following Martin's lead, prefers to keep its shareholders in the dark.

> Instead of facilitating an honest debate among Canadians about how available resources should most effectively be allocated, and to what priorities, Finance officials expend more energy trying to convince Canadians that those resources are not even there.

THERE IS NO DENYING THAT CANADA'S FISCAL SITUATION IS dramatically healthier today than when Martin was appointed Finance Minister in the new Liberal government of Jean Chrétien. Large chronic deficits have been replaced by consistent (if manipulated) surpluses. More importantly, the debt burden has been dramatically reduced, and this opens up billions of dollars annually in new fiscal room for the federal government (as debt service costs shrink steadily in importance). Martin deserves fair credit for how he prepared Canadians to take on the tough, unavoidable task of deficit-reduction. At the same time, however, he made certain choices that have proven to be unnecessary and imprudent. His deficit-reduction timetable (the real one, not the "official" one) was far more accelerated than it needed to be.

His strategy featured a damaging focus on program spending cutbacks that most other industrialized countries (even those with worse deficits to start with) avoided. His fiscal choices once the deficit was eliminated favoured the high-income households and corporations that have captured the majority of tax savings – even though they bore the least of the economic and social burden of deficit reduction. And his efforts to inject deliberate but misleading fiscal cushions into the budgeting process have resulted in a situation in which federal budgets are as non-transparent and manipulative as they have ever been (albeit in a direction which suits the powerful financial interests who used to criticize federal budgets so energetically).

In short, Martin's fiscal and political legacy in the realm of federal budgeting is much more complex than is usually described. Yes, he is the Finance Minister who slew the deficit dragon. But he did it in a particular way, for which we are still paying the costs. Perhaps we can hope that, as Prime Minister, Martin will commit to running a more balanced, and a more honest, fiscal shop.◣◢

Notes

[1] Total federal spending fell more rapidly immediately after the conclusion of World War II, due to the completion of the war effort.

[2] The data in Figure 1 include provincial deficits for comparability between countries; the federal deficit accounted for about three-quarters of the total.

[3] The one exception to this general pattern (not portrayed on Figure 1) is Japan, which began the 1990s with significant surpluses but then incurred large deficits later in the decade due to its protracted recession.

4   Repeated editions of the Alternate Federal Budget argued that lower interest rates and more expansionary macroeconomic policy were crucial to reducing deficits, and this view proved to be correct in practice.

5   The projections in Figure 3 assume 5% annual growth in *nominal* GDP (the sum of real GDP growth plus inflation).

6   In fact, there are economic reasons why government may indeed want to stabilize its indebtedness at some moderate level. Highly secure government bonds play an important role in financial markets. Pension funds and individual investors generally desire to hold significant amounts of secure and liquid government bonds at the core of their portfolios to stabilize returns (especially given the volatility of stock markets). No financial asset is considered more secure in Canada than federal bonds; so the federal government needs to continue be indebted (at some level that stays constant relative to the overall volume of financial wealth) to be able to supply these bonds in accordance with this demand.

7   In the event of a recession, of course, the debt/GDP ratio would grow more quickly in the presence of a small deficit, simply because the denominator (nominal GDP) is expanding much more slowly, or may (in a serious case) be stagnant. To maintain stability in the debt ratio over a whole business cycle, then, the government might want to target smaller deficits (i.e., less than the illustrated 2% of GDP) during years of economic expansion.

8   It was for this reason, for example, that the Alternative Federal Budget accepted the need to eliminate the deficit in the mid-1990s – although it set out to accomplish this goal in a more balanced and gradual manner than did Finance Minister Martin.

9   As already has been proven in several provinces, however, these "laws" are easily overridden when governments of the day find it politically convenient to do so. The fact that the largest provincial deficits in recent years have been incurred by hard-right governments in Ontario and B.C. is further evidence that this newfound "anti-deficit religion" was not especially lasting, at least at the provincial level.

10 The pledge to never incur a deficit also raises an important issue regarding the federal government's large accumulated Employment Insurance surplus. The government has justified this surplus on grounds that it may be needed to cover benefit costs during some future economic downturn; yet the government simultaneously promises to never again incur a deficit in its overall budget balance (which includes the EI fund). The only way these two statements are compatible is if the federal government offset a recession-induced deficit in its EI program with a large surplus on all other programs – a situation which is difficult to envision in the middle of a recession. What this contradictory position actually reveals is that the federal government has no intention of ever spending the tens of billions of dollars it has

accumulated in the EI account as a result of the dramatic reductions in benefit eligibility in the 1990s.

[11] An earlier version of Table 2 was published by the author in "The Economic and Social Consequences of Fiscal Retrenchment in Canada in the 1990s," *Review of Economic Performance and Social Progress* 1, 2001.

[12] In other words, it is assumed that each dollar of reduced program spending translated into a reduced dollar of GDP; no additional spin-off (multiplier effects) are assumed.

[13] Indeed, by 1999 the government could have increased nominal program spending by $6 billion and still balanced the budget, as indicated in Table 2.

[14] Even simply by freezing nominal program spending at its 1994 level, federal program spending would still have declined by 1.8 points of GDP between 1994 and 1997 (about half the actual decline which occurred during this time).

[15] In practice, Ottawa has tended to overestimate its planned program spending during this time, and then made up for the difference (on average over the nine years) with year-end spending announcements which exhausted some of the surplus funds which otherwise would have existed. Excluding these year-end announcements, the overestimation of program costs provided another source of financial cushion in the budgets.

[16] While market interest rates can be volatile at times, most of the government's debt is financed through longer-term instruments whose servicing costs are known in advance and do not reflect transitory ups and downs in financial markets.

⁐

CHAPTER 3

Taxation: The Martin Record

by Hugh Mackenzie

On October 18, 2000, Paul Martin rose from his seat next to the Prime Minister in the House of Commons to deliver an election budget that cut federal taxes by $100 billion over five years. In that political moment, the campaign of the newly-formed Canadian Alliance all but vanished, the core of their platform appearing plank after plank in the self-satisfied drone of the Minister of Finance.

But the Alliance Party's platform wasn't all that vanished on October 18, 2000.

So did the hopes of progressives within the Liberal party, and without, for a renewal any time soon of the federal government's role in Canadian social policy. One wonders if any of the Liberals who leaped to their feet to applaud this "political master-stroke" understood that their efforts to restore public services devastated by the fight against the deficit had just been dealt a body blow. One wonders if the Prime Minister sitting beaming up at his Minister of Finance appreciated that this budget would force him into an embarrassing last-minute struggle to rehabilitate his legacy and to distinguish it from that of his bitter internal rival.

Having decimated public services in his crusade against the deficit, Paul Martin had with one stroke wiped out the government's fiscal capacity to rebuild the services and transfers that were cut in the mid-1990s. His tax policy "coup" etched in stone his vision of a smaller, less influential federal government in a way that none of his actions in the previous five years could have done.

Reducing fiscal capacity was the main event, but, in any other political atmosphere, the side-effects would have been just as worthy of note. Martin's move to slash capital gains taxes – in effect conferring a substantial tax preference on unearned income – drove the final nail into the coffin of the 1960s Carter Commission notion that "a buck is a buck is a buck" that underpinned the goals of Canadian tax reform for thirty years. That move also put the finishing touches on a tax plan so disproportionate in its favouring of the highest-income taxpayers that it would have made Brian Mulroney's notoriously pro-business Finance Minister, Michael Wilson, blush.

And by embarking on a program of substantial corporate tax cuts, Martin abandoned Canada's resistance to pressure from tax cutters in the United States and vaulted to the head of the pack in the race to the bottom in the taxation of income from capital.

Cutting off the life support for public services renewal

Of course, the package of tax cuts announced by Martin in October 2000 was not the first tax change he made, nor was reducing federal fiscal capacity the only tax policy objective on his agenda. But to understand the significance of Martin's tax package, you have to go back five years to the beginning of his five-year quest to reduce and then control the size of the federal government – the one clear accomplishment of Martin's career as Finance Minister.

When Paul Martin officially unveiled his assault on the federal public economy in his 1995 budget speech, one of his many forecasts stood out from the others:

> By 1996-97, we will have reduced program spending from $120 billion in 1993-94 to under $108 billion. Relative to the size of our economy, program spending will be lower in 1996-97 than at any time since 1951.[1] [emphasis added]

It was a forecast breathtaking in its simplicity and stunning in its implications. And, in true Paul Martin fashion, it was understated. Federal program spending for the 1996-7 fiscal year turned out to be 12.5% of GDP – lower than in any budget year since 1949-50. Even with the so-called "spending spree" with which Jean Chrétien ended his period as Prime Minister, the government's current forecasts have spending stabilizing at 11.6% of GDP.[2] We've only had two years since 1940 with a smaller federal government role in the economy: 1947-8 and 2000-1.

To find a point of comparison for Martin's vision of the role of the federal government in the economic lives of Canadians, he took Canadians back in our history to before Medicare, before the Canada Assistance Plan, before the Quiet Revolution in Quebec, before the era of co-operative federalism, before CBC Television first went on the air – in short, to an era before the beginnings of the development of the modern Canadian nation state.

At the time of Martin's 1995 budget, this unprecedented assault on Canadian public services was excused as a necessary response to an intractable federal budgetary deficit – as a *temporary* sacrifice on the part of all Canadians in order to secure our economic future. With the benefit of hindsight, we know that the deficit was largely a cyclical phenomenon – that, in the period of economic growth and reduced interest rates in the late 1990s, the budget would have been balanced ahead of Martin's original timetable without any program spending cuts. We also know, with the benefit of hindsight, that the sacrifice was neither temporary nor shared. Most of the essays in this book are devoted to an exploration of these facts.

By embarking on a program of substantial corporate tax cuts, Martin abandoned Canada's resistance to pressure from tax cutters in the U.S. and vaulted to the head of the pack in the race to the bottom in the taxation of income from capital.

We now know that the deficit justification was a fraud; that Paul Martin seized on Canadians' concern for their country's fiscal health as a smokescreen behind which he drove the Government of Canada towards a vision of a radically reduced role for public services in the lives of Canadians.

The crusade against the deficit served Martin's vision of smaller government well. But it could not last. The once-intractable deficit melted away so quickly that Martin had to resort to laughably blatant underestimates of revenue and overstatements of expenditures to dampen Canadians' expectations of an end to their "temporary" sacrifices. By 1997, the threat that the deficit might actually be beaten was so grave that Martin understated revenue by $20 billion in an effort to keep resumed spending growth off the agenda for that year's federal election.

Revenue growth was accelerating rapidly, even as program cuts announced by Martin in the mid-1990s were still being implemented. Bur-

Table 1: Revenue and Program Spending, 2001-1 (actual) to 2008-9 (forecast) – millions of dollars

		2000-1	2001-2	2002-03	2003-04	2004-05	2005-06	2006-07	2007-08	2008-09
TAX REVENUES	Personal income tax	82,300	83,790	81,707	83,440	86,025	91,105	96,200	102,375	109,530'
	Corporate income tax	28,200	24,013	22,222	23,450	24,755	26,095	26,855	26,990	26,860
	Other income tax	4,300	3,035	3,291	3,315	3,455	3,585	3,710	3,825	3,895
	Total income tax	114,800	110,838	107,220	110,205	114,235	120,785	126,765	133,191	140,285
	Goods and services tax	25,000	24,909	28,248	29,260	31,170	32,865	34,585	36,425	38,475
	Customs import duties	2,800	3,018	3,221	3,130	3,440	3,915	4,225	4,445	4,710
	Energy taxes	4,758	2,496	2,525	2,585	2,650	2,700	2,735	2,775	
	Other excise taxes/duties	8,300	3,953	6,971	6,920	7,080	7,235	7,380	7,550	7,815
	Air Travellers Security Charge	421	375	395	415	430	445	460		
	Total	36,100	36,638	41,357	42,210	44,670	47,080	49,320	51,600	54,235
	Total tax revenues	151,000	147,476	148,577	152,415	158,905	167,865	176,085	184,790	194,520
	EI premium revenues	18,700	17,980	17,870	17,500	17,135	16,965	17,420	18,035	18,730
	Other revenues	8,900	7,859	11,115	10,575	10,250	10,700	10,850	11,100	11,330
	Total budgetary revenues	178,600	173,315	177,562	180,490	186,290	195,530	204,355	213,925	224,580
PER CENT OF GDP	Personal income tax	7.8	7.7	7.1	6.9	6.8	6.8	6.9	7.0	7.1
	Corporate income tax	2.7	2.2	1.9	1.9	1.9	2.0	1.9	1.8	1.7
	Goods and services tax	2.4	2.3	2.4	2.4	2.5	2.5	2.5	2.5	2.5
	Other excise	1.1	1.1	1.1	1.1	1.1	1.1	1.0	1.0	1.0
	Tax revenues	14.3	13.5	12.9	12.5	12.5	12.6	12.5	12.6	12.6
	EI premium revenues	1.8	1.6	1.5	1.4	1.3	1.3	1.2	1.2	1.2
	Non-tax revenues	0.8	0.7	1.0	0.9	0.8	0.8	0.8	0.8	0.7
	Total	16.9	15.9	15.4	14.8	14.7	14.6	14.6	14.5	14.6
TAX CUTS	Personal income tax	6,200	12,700	15,600	18,300	22,300				
	Corporate income tax	-	600	1,900	3,200	4,400				
	Employment insurance	1,500	2,500	3,000	3,800	4,400				
	Total	7,700	15,900	20,500	25,300	31,100				
	Adjusted revenue	186,300	189,215	198,062	205,790	217,390	229,735	240,104	253,082	265,867
	as % of GDP	17.6%	17.4%	17.2%	16.9%	17.2%	17.2%	17.2%	17.2%	17.2%
	Tax cut losses	7,700	15,900	20,500	25,300	31,100	34,205	35,749	39,157	39,287
	as % of GDP	0.7%	1.5%	1.8%	2.1%	2.5%	2.6%	2.6%	2.7%	2.6%
	Program spending	119,300	126,700	133,323	142,050	147,064	155,310	162,575	170,361	177,890
	as % of GDP	11.3%	11.6%	11.6%	11.6%	11.6%	11.6%	11.6%	11.5%	11.6%

geoning surpluses not only destroyed the rationale for continuing with those cuts, but also confronted the government with two unpleasant facts: the Martin cuts hadn't been necessary in the first place; and the economy was generating more than enough additional revenue to make a substantial start on rebuilding.

At first, ultra-conservative economic assumptions, contingency reserves, and allowances for "prudence" kept the revenue growth off the political table until after the fiscal year-end, when it was too late to do anything with it except pay down the public debt.

So in the well-worn pattern of neo-conservative governments around the world, from Ronald Reagan and Margaret Thatcher forward, Martin set out to cut off the life-support for public services renewal by radically reducing taxes.

Seizing the opportunity presented by the demonstrated political salience of tax cuts in the province of Ontario and the imagined threat from the right in the form of the Canadian Alliance, on the eve of the 2000 election Martin pushed through a tax cut of $100 billion over five years.

As Chart 1 and Table 1 show, the impact of the tax cuts on the fiscal capacity of the Government of Canada has been dramatic. By the fifth year – 2004-5 – federal government revenue-raising capacity will be down by $31.1 billion a year, compared with where it was in 2000-1, a reduction of 17% in total federal government revenue compared with what it would

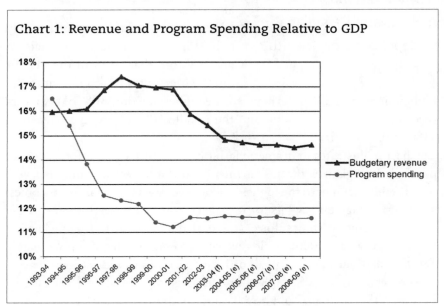

Chart 1: Revenue and Program Spending Relative to GDP

have been without the tax cuts. Measures not fully implemented by 2004-5, including the elimination of the capital tax on large corporations, will reduce revenue still further in subsequent years.

"Rewarding Canadians for their sacrifices"

Finance Minister Martin pitched his tax cuts as a "reward" to Canadians for the sacrifices they had made in the fight to eliminate the federal deficit. Fine-sounding rhetoric, except that the Canadians who were rewarded were not the Canadians who had suffered the sacrifices imposed on them through federal budget cuts. The burden of the cuts had fallen disproportionately on the poor and disabled (through the elimination of the Canada Assistance Plan); on the unemployed (as a result of substantial cuts in unemployment insurance benefits); on students (through the cuts in federal transfers to the provinces for higher education and as a result of changes to the Canada Student Loans Program); on the under-housed and homeless (as a result of the elimination of the co-operative and non-profit housing program); and on Canadians who depend on our health care system (as a consequence of a reduction of the federal share of provincial Medicare costs.

> The burden of the cuts had fallen disproportionately on the poor and disabled, the unemployed, students, the under-housed and homeless, and Canadians who depend on our health care system.

The benefits went disproportionately to the highest-income individuals in Canada. More than 30% of the benefit from the Martin tax package went to the highest-income 5.3% of taxpayers. The highest-income 30% of taxpayers received 70% of the benefit, and the middle 50% of taxpayers received 31% of the benefit.[3]

Chart 2 illustrates in dramatic fashion the nature of the Martin tax cut package. It organizes the tax savings from the lowest-income taxpayers with taxable incomes to the highest-income taxpayers with taxable incomes, showing average tax savings for taxpayers from the lowest-income to the highest-income. It shows, for example, that a taxpayer in the median income range ($30-35,000) would receive an average saving of approximately $800. A taxpayer in the top half of 1% of incomes would receive an average saving of just over $19,000. For comparison purposes, an equal distribution of the savings would be a flat line at approximately $1,100.

The area under the line on the chart measures the total value of the tax cut as we move up the income scale.

By far the most inequitable of the Martin tax moves was the reduction in the inclusion rate for capital gains from 75% to 50% – reducing the rate of tax on capital gains from 3/4 of the normal tax rate to 1/2. More than 45% of the benefit from the capital gains tax cut went to the highest income 0.6% of taxpayers. The highest-income 25% of taxpayers received nearly 90% of the benefit.

These data do not take into account tax and transfer changes based on family incomes. In particular, they do not account for improvements in the Child Tax Benefit, which provided substantial additional benefits to low-income families not dependent on social assistance, or for cuts to unemployment insurance.

However, a more complete calculation based on census families presents a similar picture. An analysis of the full package of tax-and-transfer changes based on year-2000 family incomes shows that the highest-income 23% of census families (incomes over $75,000) derived 51% of the benefit. The lowest-income 20% received 4.7% of the benefit.[4]

While the decision to cut taxes on unearned capital gains income was the most blatant assault on the "buck is a buck" philosophy that had guided Canadian tax policy for more than a generation, it was not Martin's first assault on those principles.

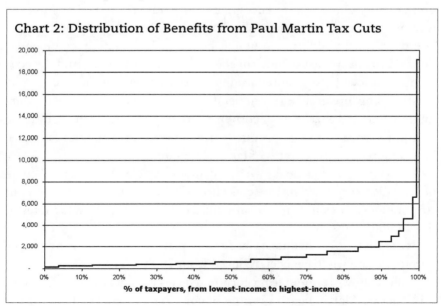

Chart 2: Distribution of Benefits from Paul Martin Tax Cuts

% of taxpayers, from lowest-income to highest-income

One of the guiding principles of Canadian tax policy had been the view that the granting of special deductions and credits in the personal income tax system undermined the equity of the tax system and destroyed its transparency. From the early 1970s on, successive federal governments had moved to limit or eliminate special categorical deductions that favoured certain types of income or expenditures over others. During Paul Martin's tenure as Finance Minister, the principle of horizontal equity – equal treatment of individuals with equal incomes – was turned on its head, as Martin moved to deliver financial assistance directly to individual Canadians through the tax system. Even during his deficit-fighter period, Martin's annual budgets were laced with narrowly-targeted tax-delivered preferences, many of them in the areas of public policy in which program spending was being most sharply curtailed.

Corporate taxes and the race to the bottom

The only significant tax-reform thinking undertaken during Paul Martin's tenure as Finance Minister was a sweeping analysis of Canadian corporate taxation conducted by then-University of Toronto Professor Jack Mintz.[5] Asked to make revenue-neutral recommendations for reform of Canada's corporate income tax system, Professor Mintz's Task Force recommended that the government eliminate a wide range of special deductions, credits, and tax preferences in the corporate tax system and use the revenue generated from their elimination to fund a reduction in corporate tax rates. In addition, although he made no specific recommendations, Mintz expressed skepticism about the policy case for – and the economic efficacy of – special reduced tax rates for small businesses.

Mintz's tax preference recommendations were ignored. Instead, Martin implemented a package of corporate tax cuts that put Canada into the lead in the race to the bottom in North America in corporate tax rates, including reductions in rates of tax on small businesses.

The Ministry of Finance's own data demonstrate clearly that the schedule of Canadian corporate tax rate cuts currently being implemented will put corporate tax rates in Canada substantially below corporate tax rates in the United States.

By the time the schedule of cuts is complete in 2008, the general corporate tax rate will have been reduced from 28% to 21%.

Table 1 shows revenue from corporate taxes dropping from 2.7%% of GDP before Martin began his orgy of corporate tax cuts to 1.7% by the end of the federal government's current five-year planning horizon. Relative to the size of the economy, corporate taxes will have been cut by more than 35% by 2008-9.

For all the talk about having to respond to a competitive taxation environment, Canada is now a source of negative pressure on public revenue from corporations in other jurisdictions. We are well ahead in the race to the bottom. It's a race you join by reducing the contribution made by the owners of corporations to the support of public services. A race in which you move ahead by giving in more, and more quickly, to the demands of corporations for a free ride. A race in which your lead inevitably evaporates, as other jurisdictions are forced to bid corporate taxes even lower.

Looking forward

Paul Martin likes to use words of caution in describing his approach to politics: words like balance; responsibility; prudence. And during his period as Finance Minister, he structured his budgets, and his forecasts of their impact, so that they appeared to support that claim.

In fact, the Finance Minister was anything but cautious in delivering

> For all the talk about having to respond to a competitive taxation environment, Canada is now a source of negative pressure on public revenue from corporations in other jurisdictions. We are well ahead in the race to the bottom.

on the wish lists of the most conservative forces in Canadian society.

By his own proud admission, he reduced federal public service to its level in the late 1940s. And, through his tax policies, he made it next-to-impossible for any centrist government to recover the ground lost.

So don't expect to see any true initiatives on the tax side from Paul Martin. As Prime Minister, he will follow the pattern he set as Finance Minister, implementing tax cuts as they are needed to slow revenue growth down to the pace of expenditure growth in a constrained and still-shrinking federal government.

That doesn't mean we won't see more tax cuts from Paul Martin. He has made it clear repeatedly that he intends to continue to cut Canada's revenue potential to fit a (reduced) program spending level. That message is reinforced by his repeated declaration that his first step towards implementing any new agenda items will be to find space within the existing budget through program review.

That begs two questions: where might the potential cuts come from? And where will the political will come from to implement them?

Health care clearly cannot be on the agenda for future spending cuts. Indeed, it is already scheduled for increases into the future, and will likely increase still further as the federal government attempts to re-establish the position in national health care policy it lost under Mulroney and Martin as Finance Minister. Nor can defence, or public security. If anything, Martin is a critic of the Chrétien government from the other side of the debate on defence spending and spending on public security. Old Age Security can't be touched. Even Paul Martin would have to acknowledge that it would be difficult to cut Employment Insurance any further.

That leaves an array of much smaller programs on the chopping block. And here, what we should expect depends on which of two Paul Martins has become the Prime Minister. Paul Martin the business turn-around artist abandoned sailors in foreign ports when his ships were re-flagged and single-handedly shut down the Great Lakes shipbuilding industry, laying off hundreds in the process. With that Paul Martin as Prime Minister, we might see entire activities of the federal government terminated. However, we have seen only occasional glimpses of that Paul Martin: when he gutted the Unemployment Insurance program; and when he tore up 25 years of federal-provincial financial arrangements with the Canada Health and Social Transfer.

Paul Martin the Finance Minister made most of his cuts by following the path of least resistance, cutting transfer payments – forcing others to do the dirty work; focusing on programs whose political constituencies didn't matter to him; and otherwise imposing small cuts across the whole federal public service. The problem is that we've been there, done that.

The question of political will is truly an unknown. In the Martin-as-Finance-Minister era, he had Jean Chrétien the disarming salesman standing in front of him, convincing Canadians of the need to make "tough choices" and creating the political space within which Martin could work. Chrétien had a reserve of public affection to draw on. There is no evidence that Martin has a similar reserve. And there is no evidence that

Martin has the communications skills to sell more cutbacks at a time when there is no perceived crisis that calls for them.

Notes

[1] Budget Speech, 1995.

[2] Fiscal and Economic Update, Annex 3, p. 103

[3] Estimates of impact derived from a model of the Canadian tax system using the most current available personal income tax data (2001). In the model, detailed tax form data for income groups are used to simulate revenue raised under various rate-and-tax-credit structures. Source Data: Individual Income Tax Statistics, Interim Basic Table 2A, Taxable Returns by Total Income Class.

[4] Analysis of the impact of Federal Government tax and transfer policy changes announced in the 2000 Budget and Mini-Budget, using the Social Policy Simulation Database and Model, Version 7.0.

[5] Professor Mintz is currently on leave from the University of Toronto as President of the C.D. Howe Institute.

CHAPTER 4

Intergovernmental Finance

by Todd Scarth

One of the first public images of Paul Martin after his near-acclamation as Liberal leader was of him palling around with the provincial premiers and territorial leaders at the Grey Cup. It was an odd image, in part because it seemed lifted out of a slightly quaint and fogey-ish earlier time, largely because it was not long ago that the provinces were in a rage at the federal government as a result of the cuts to transfers that Martin engineered while Finance Minister. Together with his much-ballyhooed "new deal for cities," the Grey Cup get-together, where the main subject of conversation was health care, demonstrated the emphasis Martin intends to put on the issue of intergovernmental relations.

There is good reason for him to want to improve relations with the provinces, as federal-provincial relations are highly strained. (And health care is the fulcrum on which they balance.) So Martin is starting from a difficult position, but he is unlikely to receive much sympathy. More than anyone, Martin is responsible for poisoning the well of federal-provincial relations. While he was Minister of Finance, he oversaw major cuts and changes to the way that the federal government transfers funds to the provinces to provide social programs.

It is almost certain that, when it comes to intergovernmental affairs, Martin really will be different from his predecessor. Jean Chrétien appeared satisfied to have reached a kind of stalemate with the provinces, in which he clung to a ragged version of the post-Trudeau Liberals' ideal of a strong central government, while the provinces used him as a whipping-boy over health funding. After watching their beloved public health care system endure a decade-long stretch of crises and cuts, Canadians were weary of this situation, and wary of the views expressed by both sides. And for the most part both deserved this mistrust.

Federal-provincial transfers had been cut sharply in the 1990s, and had rebounded only sluggishly in the post-deficit era. Many provinces determinedly pushed ahead with dangerous privatization, facilitated by a decentralization of powers. When a 16-year-old drives too fast and smashes up the family car, who do you blame – him, or his parents for giving him the keys? In the fall of 2003, the Centre for Research and Information on Canada released a poll that found that, when asked which level of government they most trusted to safeguard health care, one in three Canadians answered "neither."[1]

Being able to take credit for improving cooperation between the federal and provincial governments would be a real political prize, and Martin seems determined to claim it. It is central to his promise of delivering "change." But his policy legacy suggests that the "change" he delivers, far from a backing down from the transformations of the 1990s, may actually take the form of an intensification of these measures, where national standards and values will continue to be actively dismantled as they are pushed through the meat grinder of "program review."

The drastic overhaul in the way the federal government finances and delivers programs was begun with Martin's 1995 budget, and the introduction of the Canada Health and Social Transfer (CHST), which took effect in 1996. The seven subsequent budgets were essentially amplifications of the principles set out in 1995.

The CHST's predecessors, the Canada Assistance Plan and the Established Programs Financing for Health, had been shared-cost programs, and thus allowed the federal government a good deal of influence over provincial policies. Because the CHST is a block funding mechanism, with federal funding for welfare and social services combined in a single fund with Medicare and post-secondary education, the federal government relinquished the ability to influence how its contribution was spent.

Despite its far-reaching effects, the CHST's most immediate role was as little more than a cost-cutting measure. The two transfers it replaced provided substantially more in total than the CHST when it was introduced. The trade-off for these cuts was a cutting of the strings that historically had allowed the feral government to enforce national standards for key programs. This was the bone tossed to the provinces. The effects of this "no-strings-attached" approach were felt quickly. It freed the provinces from having to meet a certain level of national standards, such as the requirement that they provide for those in need. The National Council of Welfare, a citizens' advisory body to the Minister of Human Resources Development Canada, called the decision to kill CAP and the switch to the CHST "the worst social policy initiative undertaken by the federal government in more than a generation."[2]

Some provinces, notably Alberta and Ontario, used the opportunity to aggressively pursue the privatization of health care and the implementation of workfare programs. All provinces and territories, to one degree or another, put the squeeze on social assistance recipients, with the tacit support of the federal government. Alberta, British Columbia, and Ontario began to argue that the solution to Medicare's problems rested in transferring the delivery of health care services to the private, for-profit sector. In Alberta, legislation was passed that allowed for-profit facilities to perform surgeries requiring overnight stays.

The legal means for preventing such an erosion of Medicare's principles is the Canada Health Act, and the responsibility for enforcing it falls to the federal government. By 2002, the Auditor- General was criticizing the federal government for not abiding by its own legislation.

In 1995-96, the last year of CAP, the provinces spent 42% of this total federal transfer on health, 13% on post-secondary education, and 45% on social assistance. No one really knows how the provinces are spending the CHST dollars they receive. By all indications, the provinces are now doing only the very minimum in the way of reporting on their spending. While by doing so they are in a sense asserting their rights under the new funding arrangements, this makes the development of meaningful indicators much more difficult. And, while the federal government may prefer to have better reporting, it apparently feels no pressure to change as a result of the present reality. Rather, it has continued to implement new programs, such as the Millennium Scholarships, that provide funding directly to individuals.

What we do know is that health care is the fastest-growing (and largest) share of most provincial budgets, and therefore the proportion of CHST money dedicated to social assistance or education has fallen since the program was introduced. It could be argued that health care is the top priority for Canadians, and so there is nothing wrong with this situation. But the lack of transparency is bizarre and makes progressive health care reform wildly difficult.

By 2000, the federal government was regularly booking large budgetary surpluses. Most provinces (with the particular exception of oil-rich Alberta) were not. In September 2000, the Prime Minister and the Premiers agreed to an accord in which the federal government agreed to increase funding over five years by committing $18.9 billion in new funds.

One bizarre feature of the CHST is that its funding formula allows increases in overall federal support from year to year, based on increases in the gross domestic product (GDP). This model assumes that the cost of welfare and social services will increase more or less in line with the economy as a whole. However, welfare has traditionally been a "counter-cyclical" social program; when the economy is weak and unemployment high, demand for assistance through the program grows. Linking funding to the GDP was also inappropriate for social services, which were far less developed than any of the other three programs. Childcare, for example, is still the least developed part of the social safety net in most parts of Canada, but potentially one of the more expensive programs.

The CHST does not automatically cover 50% of social assistance costs incurred by provinces. The loss of cost-sharing also meant the end of one of the key "automatic stabilizers" that had helped earlier governments smoothe out the shocks of an economic downturn. When the economy slows, and unemployment rises, more people are forced onto social assistance. Under the old cost-sharing arrangement, the federal contribution to social assistance would kick in and money would automatically flow to those who were suffering the brunt of rising unemployment and reduced wages. This mechanism, which provided some fiscal stimulus without requiring new legislation – or even that government recognize the problem – is now gone.

When new programs were introduced, they were fundamentally different from their predecessors, as the federal government's impotence to shape provincial programs was institutionalized. The National Child Benefit, for example, was designed with heavy input from Finance. It goes over the heads of the provinces, and relies on the tax system as a delivery mechanism. The trade-off is that the federal government's role is explicitly limited to providing income to families directly, through the Canada Child Tax Benefit and the National Child Benefit Supplement. Programs and services for families and children are now completely in the hands of the provinces and territories.

Was this a fair trade for the provinces? No.

Martin cut overall transfers to the provinces, but attempted to buy them off by freeing them of conditionality. Martin's true legacy in this area is that, even as federal finances allow (and political pressures dictate) an increase in federal transfers to the provinces, such increases will not automatically be accompanied by a return to national standards. The February 2003 First Ministers' meeting, at which a new health accord was hammered out, saw the provinces agree to relinquish some of their autonomy through the creation of a Health Council, as recommended by the Romanow Commission months earlier (Alberta and Quebec both continue to resist this return to a slightly stronger federal role in determining how provinces spend health dollars). Yet keep in mind that even this patchwork measure was achieved after Martin was out of the cabinet.

There are numerous other examples of how changes to the financing and delivery of transfers to the provinces, wrought by Martin while in Finance, leave a legacy of a weaker social safety net, even when federal dollars start to flow again.

In 1993, the federal government abdicated all responsibility for new social housing, canceling its funding altogether. Not surprisingly, Canada now faces a housing crisis. In November 2001, the federal government agreed with the provincial and territorial ministers on a Framework for the funding of affordable housing. This, too, stands as an example of failed federal-provincial fiscal arrangements enacted when Martin was Minister of Finance. The federal government committed to a total potential contribution of $680 million over five years – but based funding on the willingness of provinces to provide matching funds. In May 2002, the National Housing and Homelessness Network released a report card on the Framework. It gave the federal government a D- for spending only a tiny fraction — less than 1% — of the potential funds.

Similarly, for nearly five years the federal government has attempted to put some new resources into early childhood development. Yet each advance has run up against provincial unwillingness to abide by federal priorities, with the Ontario government in particular refusing to spend Early Childhood Development Initiatives funds on programs such as child care.

Martin set the stage for years of intense federal-provincial bickering over health dollars. And the cuts to overall transfers left most provinces cutting key social programs, downloading responsibility for such programs onto municipal governments (who were even less able to afford them), or both. As a result, one legacy of Martin's time in Finance is weaker municipal services, even in areas that do not fall under federal jurisdiction, such as municipal infrastructure. In his campaign to replace Chrétien as Liberal leader, Paul Martin pointed to only two or three major policy positions that distinguished him from Chrétien. One of these is the "new deal for cities." As Finance Minister, Martin engineered the spending cuts and offloading that threw cities into crisis. Martin is now dining out on a promise to solve a crisis that he, more than anyone, created.

It is too early to know what this new deal will look like. Will Martin continue to go over the heads of the provinces and provide the bulk of new funding to cities? Will the support merely take the form of cash – welcome but on its own insufficient – or will Martin make a place for municipal leaders at the table currently occupied only by the federal and provincial representatives? With the political momentum that has built up behind support for municipal infrastructure, Martin could use it to provide the leverage needed to re-assert the federal government's role in shaping provincial programs.

If Martin were able to bring to an end the circular bickering over health care funding and the spending cuts and off-loading that characterized intergovernmental fiscal relations in the 1990s, that would be a step forward. But, given his past, Martin's eagerness to make federal-provincial relations friendlier is also somewhat troubling. The social safety net that was so weakened in the 1990s needs dramatic reinvestment of public funds, as well as a strong federal government, to protect and rebuild it. The recent pattern of trading off one of these for the other could be disastrous, and it was Martin who did more than anyone to establish that pattern. If, at the next Grey Cup health meeting, Ralph Klein seems particularly happy, Canadians should not be too surprised – but they should be worried.❧

Note

[1] Jenson, Jane. "Will the Prime Minister Displace the Finance Minister? Paul Martin's Social Policy for a 'New Era.'" *Policy Options*. December 2003 – January 2004.

꒰

CHAPTER 5

Paul Martin's Economic Record

Living Standards of Working Families and Prospects for Future Prosperity

by Andrew Jackson

It is transparently absurd to give all of the credit or blame for Canada's economic performance between 1993 and 2002 to the then incumbent Minister of Finance. Nonetheless, for better or worse, Paul Martin was the single major architect of economic policy over this period, and the policies for which he was responsible did shape key outcomes.

Martin had the great good fortune to take over as the Canadian economy was starting to recover from the severe downturn of the late 1980s and early 1990s, and he had the good sense not to re-appoint John Crow as Governor of the Bank of Canada. Under the impetus of falling interest rates, a depreciating Canadian dollar, and a booming U.S. economy, economic growth gathered pace after 1992. The strong recovery was dampened through the mid- to late 1990s by the effect of Martin's deep cuts to public expenditures and, at the end of the decade, by the collapse of the U.S. boom and the impacts of the Asian financial crisis on resource prices. Fortunately, by the late 1990s, the fiscal squeeze had more or less run its course, and rising Canadian family incomes fuelled domestically-driven growth. This compensated for the post-bubble U.S. and global slowdown until 2003, when then Finance Minister John Manley saw growth slow to a snail's pace.

Martin can, and does, point to a record of strong economic growth and rising employment during his watch. Indeed, by the key measure of growth of real GDP per person, Canada put in just about the strongest economic performance of any major industrialized country, including the U.S.

On close examination, however, the overall economic record is flawed when viewed from the perspective of working families. As detailed below, the growth of household incomes was not anywhere near as robust as GDP growth, and was fuelled by a growth in jobs rather than by a growth in real wages. In other words, working families have mainly increased their incomes by working longer hours. The quality of jobs has not greatly improved, despite strong employment growth. And income inequality and poverty have both increased when account is taken of the state of the business cycle. Re-distributive economic transfers, economic security, and access to public and social services were all undermined by Martin's spending cuts, particularly cuts to the Employment Insurance program and transfers to the provinces.

In the famous Liberal *Red Book* of 1993, co-authored by Martin, and in successive Budget speeches, strong emphasis was placed upon boosting the new "knowledge-based" economy through strategic investments in innovation, research and development, and skills. The basic argument – which is fundamentally correct – is that Canada's role in the global economy should be as a producer of sophisticated goods and services which can command high prices and support decent jobs. After the deficit was eliminated, Martin's Budgets made major investments in the "innovation agenda." Disappointingly, however, Canada's productivity and innovation record leaves much to be desired.

Economic Growth and the Well-Being and Incomes of Canadians

The Liberals took office in 1993 just after the Canadian economy began to rebound from the deep slump of 1990-92. From 1993 through 2002, real (inflation-adjusted) annual GDP growth averaged 3.6%, peaking at more than 5% in each of 1999 and 2000. Growth per person in this period exceeded even that of the U.S. Real GDP per capita rose by a cumulative total of 26.9% between 1993 and 2002, compared to 20.9% in the U.S. Canada grew faster than the U.S. in GDP per person terms in every year except 1996 and 1997. As a result, measured at purchasing power parity (which equalizes the buying power of the two currencies), Canadian GDP per capita rose from 81.3% of the U.S. level in 1993 to 86.0% in 2002. *(See Statistics Canada data posted at «www.csls.ca».)* In short, under Paul Martin's stewardship, economic growth outpaced even that of the U.S. through the late 1990s boom, and Canada managed to escape the mild U.S. recession which followed.

While real GDP growth figures are the headline numbers for economic performance, it has to be borne in mind that GDP is a very incomplete measure of economic well-being. GDP growth tells us nothing about the extent of economic and social security, though income transfers and public and social services could be improved by higher GDP. Economic growth tells us nothing about the distribution of income, not to mention the quality of life in communities, or the state of the environment.

It turns out that, for Canada in recent years, solid GDP growth is also a misleading indicator of the growth of personal and household incomes. While the GDP growth numbers have been impressive, it is striking that income in the hands of households failed to grow at anywhere near the same pace. Real GDP per person grew by 26.9% between 1993 and 2002, but real personal income per person rose by just 11.5% over this period, or by an average of only about 1% per year. Real personal income is the total of all before-tax wage, investment, small business, and government transfer income going to households, adjusted for increases in consumer prices.

Martin can, and does, point to a record of strong economic growth and rising employment during his watch. On close examination, however, the overall economic record is flawed when viewed from the perspective of working families.

There are two major reasons why real income in the hands of Canadian families has failed to grow at anywhere near the same rapid pace as real GDP. (Another reason is that consumer prices rose a bit faster than the all-price measure used to calculate real GDP.) First, government income transfers to households fell sharply as a proportion of national income. Thus, gains in labour income from higher employment were, in the aggregate, offset by lower income transfers to households from all levels of government. Second, corporate pre-tax profits have grown as a share of national income at the expense of wages and salaries.

Declining Transfers to Working-Age Households

Under Martin's tenure, the total of all government transfers to persons fell sharply, from 13.5% of GDP to 10.5% of GDP – the equivalent of $35 billion in 2002. Seniors' benefits were largely unaffected by policy changes, and rose due to population aging. But government transfers to working-age households – mainly EI and social assistance benefits – fell sharply.

Both EI and welfare benefits fell in dollar terms because of falling unemployment, which is a good thing. But the cut to EI benefits, for which Martin must take direct responsibility, had a big negative impact on spending as well. In 1993, there were 1.6 million unemployed workers on average over the year, 57% of whom collected regular EI benefits. By 2002, the number of unemployed had fallen to 1.3 million, but just 38% of the unemployed now qualified for benefits. The dollar saving was much greater than that justified by the fall in unemployment, and the cost was borne directly by the unemployed (who tend to live in lower and middle-income households).

While changes in the proportion of the unemployed eligible for EI benefits reflected to some degree a change in the make-up of the unemployed population, such as more new entrants to the workforce, the sharp decline in the proportion of the unemployed collecting benefits mainly reflected the shift to an hours-based system with higher qualifying periods of work. This heavily penalized many (mainly women) seasonal, casual, and part-time workers, compared to the 1993 system.

Martin must also take responsibility for changes to federal child benefits. The re-design of the system, notably the introduction of the National Child Benefit, resulted in higher benefits for some low-income working families with children, but, by design, did not provide an income supplement for the many low-income families with children on provincial social welfare programs. Martin cannot, perhaps, be directly blamed for deep welfare cuts in the two richest provinces of Alberta and Ontario, especially since provincial governments there chose to deliver tax cuts. But cuts to provincial transfers and the elimination of 50/50 federal cost-sharing of welfare under the Canada Assistance Plan certainly pushed the costs of social assistance (and related social programs such as child care) onto the provinces, including provinces which had little fiscal room to manoeuvre. No province increased welfare rates at anything near the rate of inflation after the mid-1990s, resulting in deep income cuts to Canada's poorest households. Welfare cuts fell not just on persons and families outside the workforce, but also on the working poor who move between low-wage jobs and social assistance.

To summarize, while GDP growth was strong in the 1990s and did raise incomes from work as unemployment fell, the impact on incomes of working-age households was significantly offset by cuts to EI and social assistance programs. As noted below, this shows up in the very modest income growth of low to modest income families in the Martin era.

Rising Corporate Profits

The second major reason why personal incomes failed to match GDP growth is because corporate profits (which do not appear in personal income until distributed as investment income) rose sharply as a share of GDP in the Martin era. Between 1993 and 2002, total labour income (all wages and salaries) rose by 50%, while corporate pre-tax profits trebled, rising from $41 billion to $133 billion. As a proportion of GDP, corporate profits peaked in the 1980s' expansion at 10.6% of GDP in 1988. They bottomed out at just 4.7% of GDP in 1992, rose more or less steadily to a new, higher peak of 12.6% in 2000, before falling off a bit to 11.5% in each of 2001 and 2002. This was still well above the peak of the previous period of economic expansion. There has been a significant structural as well as cyclical increase in corporate profitability, which Bay Street seems more than willing to credit in good part to Martin (who, of course, cut taxes on surging corporate profits, as well).

Soaring Household Debt

The limited growth of personal incomes under Paul Martin might have held back household spending on consumer goods and on housing had it not been for a very sharp decline in the personal saving rate. Canadian households saved between 10% and 15% of their incomes from the mid-1970s through to the early 1990s, but the savings rate fell from 11.9% in 1993 to historic lows of less than 5% from 1997 on, and fell to a new low of 4.2% in 2002. By 2002, the average Canadian household held consumer and mortgage debt equal to 98% of their after-tax income, up from 85% in 1993. This is an historic high which could prove painful when interest rates rise from current very low levels. Average debt figures conceal the fact that many affluent older households hold little debt, which tends to be concentrated among heavily mortgaged younger families. It is interesting to note that soaring household debt has been the flip side of mounting government surpluses.

Employment, Unemployment and Job Quality

Table 1 provides some basic labour market data for 1989, the lowest unemployment year of the 1980s, for 1993, when Martin took office, and for 2002. Changes between 1989 and 2002 can be seen as "structural" changes in the job market, as opposed to the cyclical changes which took place between 1993 and 2002.

Under Martin, the national unemployment rate fell from a 1990s high of 11.4% in 1993 to a low of just 6.8% in 2000, but then bumped back up

Table 1: Labour Market Trends			
	1989	1993	2002
Unemployment Rate			
All	7.5%	11.4%	7.7%
Men	7.4%	12.0%	8.1%
Women	7.8%	10.6%	7.1%
25+	6.7%	10.2%	6.5%
Youth 15-24	11.0%	17.1%	13.6%
Average Number of Weeks Unemployed	18.0	25.1	18.4
Employment Rate			
All	62.1%	58.0%	61.8%
25-54	78.2%	74.9%	80.2%
Part-Time Rate	16.8%	19.3%	18.7%
Composition of Employment			
Public Sector Employees	20.8%	22.0%	18.9%
Private Sector Employees	65.3%	62.3%	65.9%
Self-Employed	13.9%	15.8%	15.2%
"Own Account" Self-employed	7.2%	8.7%	9.8%

to 7.7% in 2002. Between 1993 and 2002, the employment rate for all persons aged 15 to 64 rose from 58.0% to 61.8%, and the employment rate for the core working-age population aged 25 to 54 rose sharply, from 74.9% to an all-time high of 80.2%. Between 1993 and 2002, the economy created some 2.5 million new jobs, including many new "blue collar" jobs in manufacturing and construction, which offset the recent tilt of job creation to either well-paid professional/managerial jobs, or low-paid clerical, sales, and services jobs. Women shared fully in the job gains. Clearly, the overall job creation record is very impressive.

That said, there were some flaws in the record. Young people relatively lost out, and, while the youth unemployment rate fell from 1993 to 2002, it remained at 13.6% in 2002, well above the 1989 low. Public sector jobs shrank, from 22.0% to 18.9%, as a proportion of all jobs. The proportion of the workforce in part-time jobs fell slightly from 1993 to 2002, but, at 18.7% in 2002, remained significantly above the rate in 1989. At least one in three adult part-time workers, overwhelmingly women, want but cannot find full-time jobs, and part-time jobs are much lower paid on average and provide lower benefits than do full-time jobs. Further, between 1993 and 2002, the proportion of the total workforce in "own account" self-employment rose from 8.7% to 9.8%, even though the overall incidence of self-employment fell slightly. "Own account" self-employed persons employ no other persons, and generally have very low incomes. The incidence of temporary work – seasonal work plus work on short-term contracts – rose from 11.3% in 1997 (no consistent earlier data available) to 13.0% in 2002.

There was a slight tilt towards more precarious and insecure forms of work hidden in the overall job creation record. This had disproportional impacts on women workers and workers of colour, who are much more likely to hold "precarious" jobs.

In short, there was a slight tilt towards more precarious and insecure forms of work hidden in the overall job creation record. This had disproportional impacts on women workers and workers of colour, who are much more likely to hold "precarious" jobs. (For details, see *Is Work Working for Women?* and *Is Work Working for Workers of Colour?*, available from «www.clc-ctc.ca».)

While unemployment has fallen, it has to be borne in mind that the average duration of an unemployment spell is about 18 weeks, and that many workers cycle in and out of jobs over the year. In 1999, when the unemployment rate was just over 7%, more than one in eight workers were unemployed at least once in the year. The erosion of EI has made such temporary unemployment relatively more painful.

Union protection for Canadian workers has fallen. Fully consistent data are available only from 1997, but show that private sector union density fell from 21.5% to 19.6% from 1997 to 2002 (from 26.1% to 23.8% for men, and from 16.0% to 14.5% for women), while remaining constant at 75.8% in the shrinking public sector. Union decline was most marked in the expanding manufacturing sector (36.3% to 32.4%). The erosion of union density is associated with shrinking pension and health benefits coverage, a higher incidence of low pay, and larger pay gaps between women and men and between workers of colour and all other workers. (See *"In Solidarity": The Union Advantage*.)

Stagnant Wages

While job growth has been healthy and has certainly benefited working families, it is striking that, on average, there were no real wage gains whatsoever for workers during Martin's tenure as Minister of Finance. As shown in Table 2, average weekly and average hourly earnings for all workers just about matched the increase in prices, while private sector unionized workers saw a very modest real wage gain of just 3.4% in total over the whole nine years. Real public sector union wages fell, by 1.4%, over the same period.

Table 2: Wages and Prices	
% Increase, 1993-2002	
Consumer Price Index	16.9%
Average Weekly Earnings	16.8% ($583.24 to $681.09)
Average Hourly Earnings	16.2% ($14.70 to $17.08)
Union Wages – Private Sector	20.3%
Union Wages – Public Sector	15.5%
Source: Statistics Canada *Canadian Economic Observer Histrocial Statistical Supplement.*	

Real median annual earnings did increase – by 10% – between 1993 and 2001 (from $23,028 to $25,387), but this was due to working more hours in the week and weeks in the year, rather than because of higher wages per hour or week.

Data from the *Labour Force Survey* (available only from 1997) show that the boom in job creation had no impact at all on the incidence of low pay. In 1997, 25.0% of all workers – 19.4% of men and 31.1% of women – were low paid, defined as earning less than two-thirds the median (mid-point) hourly wage. In 2002, 25.3% of workers – 19.4% of men and 31.5% of women – were low paid by the same definition. International data show that the incidence of low pay in Canada, among the advanced industrial countries, is second only to the U.S. Just 5% of workers in the Scandinavian countries are low paid by the same definition of earning less than two-thirds of the national median hourly wage.

> While job growth has been healthy and has certainly benefited working families, it is striking that, on average, there were no real wage gains whatsoever for workers during Martin's tenure as Minister of Finance.

Increasing Income Inequality

Martin's tenure as Minister of Finance was marked by a major increase in income inequality, as the gains of the economic recovery went mainly to higher income families.

Table 3 provides data on income trends in the 1990s for economic families of two persons or more. The data are in constant (inflation-adjusted) dollars. Again, data are shown for 1989, 1993 and 2001 (the most recent available) so as to show the changes when Martin was Minister of Finance, as well as the longer-term structural trend.

The first part of the Table shows trends in market income, that is, wages and salaries, plus small business and investment income, but not including income from government transfers.

It is clear that the market income gains from 1993 went disproportionately to the high end. The top 20% of families, with average market incomes of $145,580 in 2001, took 45.6% of all market income in that year, up from 44.4% in 1993, and up from 42.4% in 1989. In inflation-adjusted dollar terms (measured in 2001 dollars), the market incomes of the top

Table 3: Family Income Trends in the 1990s

	1989	1993	2001	% Change 1989-2001	% Change 1993-2001
Market Income					
Bottom Quintile	$8,969	$5,307	$8,362	-6.8%	57.6%
Second Quintile	$33,729	$29,896	$32,362	-4.1%	8.2%
Middle Quintile	$53,144	$47,235	$54,127	1.8%	14.6%
Fourth Quintile	$73,844	$68,720	$78,389	6.2%	14.1%
Top Quintile	$124,953	$118,241	$145,580	16.5%	23.1%
Shares of Market Income					
Bottom Quintile	3.0%	2.0%	2.6%		
Second Quintile	11.5%	10.1%	10.2%		
Middle Quintile	18.0%	17.7%	17.0%		
Fourth Quintile	25.1%	25.8%	24.6%		
Top Quintile	42.4%	44.4%	45.6%		
After Tax/Transfer Income					
Bottom Quintile	$20,258	$18,891	$20,721	2.3%	9.7%
Second Quintile	$35,979	$32,717	$36,830	2.4%	12.6%
Middle Quintile	$48,064	$44,738	$51,074	6.3%	14.2%
Fourth Quintile	$62,247	$58,886	$67,878	9.0%	15.3%
Top Quintile	$97,242	$91,683	$113,615	16.8%	23.9%
After Tax/Transfer Income Shares					
Bottom Quintile	7.7%	7.7%	7.1%		
Next Quintile	13.6%	13.3%	12.7%		
Middle Quintile	18.2%	18.1%	17.6%		
Next Quintile	23.6%	23.9%	23.4%		
Top Quintile	36.9%	37.1%	39.2%		

(Data are for economic families of two persons or more.) Statistics Canada, Income in Canada CD-Rom. 2001. (Constant $ 2001)

Poverty (Post Tax LICO)					
All Persons	10.0%	12.9%	10.4%		
Children	11.5%	15.7%	11.4%		
18-64	9.3%	12.3%	10.6%		
65 plus	10.9%	10.8%	7.3%		

Source: Statistics Canada. Income in Canada CD-ROM. Table T802.

fifth rose by 23.1% under Martin, much more than the other income groups with the exception of the bottom 20%. However, the bottom 20%, which is disproportionately made up of elderly families and recipients of social assistance, receives very little market income, and is mainly reliant on government transfers.

As also shown in the Table, the top 20% of families also increased their share of after-tax/after-transfer income between 1993 and 2001, from 37.1% to 39.2% of the total. The share of all other income groups, including the bottom 20%, fell. This is unusual in a period of strong economic recovery, which usually provides strong benefits to lower- and middle-income groups because of falling unemployment. In the economic recovery of the 1980s (1982 to 1989), the after-tax income share of the top 20% of families remained the same, and their share of market income increased only very slightly, from 42.0% to 42.4%. Increasing inequality reflects two broad forces pushing in the same direction. As noted, the increase in market income went mainly to the top, and the cuts in government transfers to non-elderly families fell disproportionately on lower income groups. Tax changes also contributed to greater inequality.

> The increase in market income went mainly to the top, and the cuts in government transfers to non-elderly families fell disproportionately on lower income groups. Tax changes also contributed to greater inequality.

Note that a family in the middle of the income distribution saw only a 14.6% increase in real market income over the eight years from 1993 to 2001, and a 14.1% increase in real after-tax/transfer income. A real income gain of only about 1.5% per year looks very small in comparison to the average real GDP growth rate of over 3.5% per year over the same period. The bottom 40% of families fared even worse in terms of growth of after-tax/transfer incomes. In short, there has been a major disconnect between the statistics of overall economic recovery and the incomes of ordinary working families, explained in significant part by the very unequal distribution of income gains.

The picture is slightly different when it comes to poverty rates, as measured by the after-tax low-income cutoff line. Under Martin, poverty fell significantly for all age groups, reflecting the fact that the jobs recovery did give a boost to the incomes of those at the bottom, even if their share of the overall income gain was not large and was offset by cuts to transfers. However, poverty rates for the working-age population in 2001 were still well above the level of 1989, when unemployment was at about the same level. The fact that the child poverty rate was about the same in 2001 as in 1989 is no reason for great celebration, given that this was supposed to be the decade for the elimination of child poverty.

The clear bottom line is that income inequality increased significantly in the Martin years, mainly because the increasingly unequal distribution of market income was not offset to the same extent as in the recent past by government transfers to lower income families. And poverty rates remained disturbingly high.

The Social Wage

It is widely believed – with good reason – that Canadian governments spend significantly more on social programs and public services than do U.S. governments. Redistribution of income through tax-financed income support programs and delivery of services through tax-financed public services reduce reliance on wage income alone and make Canada a more equal and inclusive society. However, the difference shrank remarkably in the Paul Martin era because of spending cuts by all levels of government in the 1990s. While Martin was directly responsible only for federal spending cuts, lower federal transfers to the provinces certainly played a major role in reduced spending at the sub-national level.

Table 4 – based on data from a research paper from the Department of Finance – details program spending differences between Canada and the U.S. in 1992 and 2001. The data are for all levels of government expressed as a share of GDP. The bottom line is that Canadian governments collectively spent 34.8% of Canadian GDP on programs in 2001, while U.S. governments spent 31.9% of GDP. The difference between the two countries fell from 10.9 percentage points of GDP in 1992 to a remarkably small difference of just 2.9 percentage points in 2001, as Canadian government spending fell by almost 10 percentage points of GDP. In short, there has been a major convergence of Canada towards the small government/high inequality/high insecurity U.S. social model.

The spending gap between the two countries is greatest for non-defense spending, at a significant 5.7 percentage points of GDP, but this is down from a much greater difference of 15.2 percentage points in 1992. Note that non-defense program spending actually increased in the U.S., while falling by almost 10 percentage points of GDP in Canada. The main differences between Canada and the U.S. are in national defense (where we spend much less), and in income security programs. Here we spend 11.0% of GDP compared to 7.1% in the U.S., but the gap has shrunk greatly since 1992. This reflects cuts to welfare and EI benefits, but also falling unemployment.

Canada now spends relatively less than the U.S. on public education, the result of recent cuts in Canada and increases in the U.S. We spend only a bit more on health (though we spend much more efficiently because of public delivery and a single-payer Medicare system). We also spend relatively more on housing and community services and recreation and culture, though these are relatively small areas of expenditure.

Table 4: Canada-U.S. Fiscal Comparisons

Change in Government Spending as % GDP

Function	1992			2001		
	US	Canada	Gap	US	Canada	Gap
Income Security	7.9	14.3	6.4	7.1	11	3.9
Housing and Community Services	0.7	1.9	1.2	0.5	1.4	0.9
Economic Affairs	3.2	5.8	2.5	3.2	3.5	0.3
Recreation and Culture	0.3	1.3	1	0.3	1	0.7
Education	5.7	7.7	2	6.2	5.9	-0.3
Health	6	7.3	1.2	6.7	7	0.4
General Public Servicer	2	2.4	0.4	1.9	1.9	0
Public Order and Safety	1.9	2.3	0.5	2.2	1.9	-0.2
National Defence	6	1.7	-4.3	4	1.2	-2.8
Total Program Spending	33.7	44.6	10.9	31.9	34.8	2.9
Non-Defence Program Spending	27.7	42.9	15.2	27.9	33.6	5.7

Source: "Government Spending in Canada and the US Department of Finance Working Paper 2003-05.

It is important to spend money wisely and efficiently, but the size of spending clearly matters as well. The Canada-U.S. difference has shrunk dramatically in the 1990s because of deep cuts to Canadian spending on social programs and public services.

Good Jobs: Building a More Productive and Innovative Economy

In the famous *Red Book* prepared for the 1993 election by Paul Martin and Chaviva Hosek, the Liberals committed themselves to building an innovative "knowledge-based economy" through higher levels of public and private investment in research and development, education, and training. It was recognized that Canadian business performance in terms of investment in innovation and training had been relatively weak. The basic message, repeated in successive government policy documents and Throne speeches, has been that Canada lags too far behind other advanced industrial countries in building the "new economy" that is required to create and sustain well-paid jobs. Ultimately, the argument goes, Canada must create jobs in industries which participate in competitive world markets by producing high-value goods and services which sell because they are unique or sophisticated rather than because they are low-cost. In a world of abundant cheap labour, it is indeed true that the long-term prosperity of Canadians depends upon building a much more technologically sophisticated economy.

As Finance Minister, Martin had a real enthusiasm for innovation policy. While the 1995 Budget cut very deeply into spending by Industry Canada (almost cutting economic development program spending in half over two years), successive Budgets slowly rebuilt from a smaller base. After the deficit was eliminated in 1997, substantial resources were invested in the granting councils which fund university research; in the National Research Council and other federal research agencies; in the Canadian Foundation for Innovation which supports university and other research infrastructure; in the development of the "information highway;" and in networks of centres of excellence. A new industrial subsidy program, Technology Partnerships Canada, gave direct federal support to research and development in targeted sectors, mainly the aerospace and defense industries. Direct public support for innovation was stacked on top of corporate research and development tax credits which are considered to be the most generous in the world.

On the education and training side of the ledger, the public investment record has been much less impressive, despite the promises of the *Red Book*. Federal transfers to the provinces for post-secondary education were deeply cut, and later increases to research funding failed to undo the damage to instructional programs. Federal expenditures on training for unemployed workers were cut, and responsibility devolved to the provinces. The rhetoric of "lifelong learning" was not translated into coherent programs which would upgrade the skills of already employed workers or promote a genuine training culture in the private sector.

The Martin approach has been a classic "supply side" innovation strategy, designed to give public sector support to Canadian businesses capable of drawing on public sector and university research and education, but doing little to directly build our innovative and productive capacities or to regulate private business investment decisions. The Achilles' heel of the approach has been the underlying weakness of Canadian industry, which has been, and remains, heavily tilted towards the production of resource-based commodities and automotive products. True, Canada has some innovative sectors – such as telecom equipment, aerospace, software, pharmaceuticals and biotech, and aerospace – but the key question is whether this base is adequate for a purely "supply-side" strategy to work.

> The Martin approach has been a classic "supply side" innovation strategy, designed to give public sector support to Canadian businesses capable of drawing on public sector and university research and education, but doing little to directly build our innovative and productive capacities or to regulate private business investment decisions.

It is now widely recognized that the apparent boom in Canadian industrial exports, production and jobs, from 1992 to 2002, was based overwhelmingly upon the steady depreciation of the Canadian dollar, rather than upon rising productivity or higher levels of innovation. Both manufacturing output and employment grew rapidly in the economic recovery between 1992 and 2002. However, manufacturing productivity growth between 1992 and 2002 was much lower than in the U.S., rising by just 17.9% compared to 51.9%. Between 1995 and 2002 – the peak years of the U.S. boom – labour productivity growth in Canadian manufacturing averaged just 0.7% per year compared to 4.2% in the U.S. Despite slower real wage growth, Canada's output share would have deteriorated very seriously had not the dollar depreciated. *(See Andrew Jackson. "Why the Big Idea is a Bad Idea." CCPA. 2003, for extensive documentation.)*

Our poor relative productivity performance is due to the long-standing structural problems of Canadian industry: too many small, undercapitalized plants; relatively low-firm investment in advanced machinery and equipment, R and D, and training; over-dependence on resources and low value-added industrial materials; and an underdeveloped advanced capital goods sector. *(See OECD Economic Survey of Canada, 2003, and Conference Board of Canada, Performance and Potential, 2003.)* In the 1990s, Canadian industry invested much less than the U.S. in machinery and equipment, especially the new information-based technologies, resulting in large differences in the quality of the capital stock. Business investment in research and development increased a bit in the 1990s, but remained at less than two-thirds the U.S. level. Business investment in worker training similarly continues to lag well behind U.S. and average OECD levels.

It is now widely recognized that the apparent boom in Canadian industrial exports, production and jobs, from 1992 to 2002, was based overwhelmingly upon the steady depreciation of the Canadian dollar, rather than upon rising productivity or higher levels of innovation.

Canadian industries in the same sector are often just about as productive as U.S. industries. We are more productive in resources and the auto industry, but we have failed to decisively move up the value-added chain. We have a relatively much smaller and less productive advanced industrial sector than the U.S. or other advanced industrial countries. Capital goods industries – producing electrical and electronic equipment such as computers and telecommunications equipment, and industrial machinery and equipment, including aerospace – account for only about one-sixth of manufacturing production, compared to more than one-third in the U.S. The research and development we perform is very heavily concentrated in these sectors. Indeed, just a handful of companies, such as Bombardier and Northern Telecom, perform most Canadian research and development.

Balanced budgets, tax cuts, deeper integration of the manufacturing sector in the North American economy, and "supply-side" industrial strategies have done little to decisively shift the structure of our industrial economy away from natural resources and relatively unsophisticated manufacturing towards the more dynamic and faster-growing "knowledge-based" industries. Machinery and equipment exports did grow somewhat more rapidly than total exports in the 1990s because of the growth of the telecom and aerospace sectors, but the energy share of our exports has also been growing fast. Resources, resource-based manufacturing, and crude industrial material production combined (i.e., agriculture and fish products, energy products, forest products, and basic industrial goods, including iron and steel and smelted minerals) still make up about 45% of all exports, down just a little in the 1990s. Resource-based commodities and basic industrial materials, such as wood and paper, minerals, and primary metal products, still account for over one-third of manufacturing sector value-added, while machinery production (machinery plus aerospace) accounts for just 17.5%, up from 12.5% at the end of the 1980s.

Despite the collapse of the high-tech bubble of the 1990s, the capital goods sector remains hugely important to the long-term economic future of advanced industrial countries, given the ongoing shift of consumer goods production to lower wage-developing countries. A strong resource-based and commodity production sector is no bad thing to the extent that it is an important source of wealth and jobs and helps sustain regional economies. The distinction between a resource-based economy and a knowledge-based economy glosses over the fact that the resource industries are increasingly technologically sophisticated. Still, the long-standing Canadian structural bias to production of commodities in capital-intensive industries carries important costs. It will be very hard to raise Canadian living standards over the long-term and create well-paid jobs if we do not shift production towards goods and services which command rising rather than falling prices in world markets. That means producing more unique or sophisticated goods and services. Our dependence on large-scale crude energy exports is particularly unwise in a world of finite conventional resources, and is environmentally unsustainable from a global perspective.

In summary, for all of the focus placed by Paul Martin on building a "knowledge-based economy," Canada has taken only small steps in that direction in recent years. This begs the question of whether much more interventionist policies – such as green industrial strategies based on subsidies, regulation, and direct public investment – are needed in place of a purely "supply-side" strategy.

Conclusions

It would be absurd to argue that the Paul Martin economic record was one of failure. Canada's recent economic performance has been impressive in terms of GDP and job growth. However, it has been less impressive when the focus is upon the living standards of working families. Incomes have improved modestly, but wages have stagnated and income inequality has greatly increased. The social wage has been cut deeply, and insecurity has risen. The Canadian economy remains weak in terms of its ability to support well-paid jobs into the future. Martin's record needs to be debated rather than uncritically celebrated, and alternative approaches need to be developed if we are to do better.🌑

A NOTE ON SOURCES:

Except as otherwise indicated, data are taken or calculated from the standard sources as reported in the 2002-03 issue of Statistics Canada's *Canadian Economic Observer Historical Statistical Supplement*.

CHAPTER 6

Paul Martin and the
Liberal Social Policy Record

by John Anderson

L ike most of the other policy areas examined in this book, social policy
was never under the exclusive direction and control of the Minister of
Finance. While in that post, however, Paul Martin played a decisive role
in determining the overall financial parameters under which social policy
was forged, both in Ottawa and the provinces. In this sense, Martin's role
in slaying the deficit dragon and handing out $100 billion in personal
income tax cuts (most of which went to high-income earners) was undoubtedly more important for social policy (in terms of its effect on federal and provincial revenues available for social programs) than any new
social policy initiatives.

Martin also played a key role in three of the most important social policy
changes of this period: 1) the termination of the Canada Assistance Plan,
and 2) the establishment of the National Child Benefit 3) the changes to
Employment Insurance, as well in the decisions on other programs such
as social housing and early childhood education.

Another measure of social policy is the framework of Canada's federation in which the provinces have vital financial, jurisdictional, and administrative responsibilities. Martin undoubtedly helped to establish the Social Union framework which remains a potentially powerful but greatly
underused mechanism for new social policy. It is significant that one of
the most popular social policy initiatives of the Chrétien-Martin era, the
maternity/paternity leave program, is in trouble from the courts in Quebec because it was not the result of negotiations with the provinces.

BEFORE EXAMINING JUST WHAT HAPPENED WITH SOCIAL policy over the last decade, it might be advisable to consider what yardsticks we could use to measure the outcomes of social policies in terms of their success or failure. I would submit that the 2001 Census, in many ways, is *the* major measuring tool for social policy in the Chrétien-Martin era. If we look at the trends over the five years from 1996-2001 on such issues as low income, many indicators did improve. However, if we compare the 2001 results to that of the 1991 Census done in the Mulroney era, we have some ability to look at what was really achieved during Martin's term as finance minister.

From 1991 to 2001, overall levels of poverty in Canada stagnated at around 16%. Child poverty even went up slightly to 18.4%. Only with seniors and lone-parent families were there some dramatic reductions, but the level of lone-parent family poverty remains intolerably high at 45.8%. The seniors' poverty level, while dropping from nearly 30% 20 years ago, remains at the national average and, in fact, is over 40% for single women seniors and over 30% for single men.

For Aboriginal peoples and visible minorities, as well as people with disabilities, poverty rates remain significantly larger. Recent immigrants and visible minorities have rates double the national average, and for some groups the rates are even greater. Black children in Toronto, for example, suffer a poverty rate of 52%. The poverty rates of Aboriginal peoples remain generally even higher.

Table 1: Individuals living on low income by age, Canada 1980, 1990 and 2000						
	Number in low income			Percentage in low income		
	1980	1990	2000	1980	1990	2000
Under 18 years	1,293,655	1,203,785	1,245,650	19.4	18.2	18.4
18 to 64 years	2,163,895	2,500,835	2,873,585	14.7	14.8	15.3
65 years and over	633,895	584,545	601,260	29.8	20.3	16.8
All age groups	4,091,440	4,289,165	4,720,490	17.4	16.2	16.2

1. All individuals living below the low-income cut-offs (see the explanation in the methodology).

2. All individuals, except those living in the Yukon, Northwest Territories, Nunavut, on Indian reserves and in institutions.

Source: Statistics Canada Census 2001

Table 2: Census families living in low income Canada, 1980, 1990 and 2000

	Number in low income			Percentage in low income		
	1980	1990	2000	1980	1990	2000
All census families	893,520	936,630	1,045,735	14.2	12.8	12.6
Couple families with no children	201,825	201,765	227,525	11.1	8.7	8.2
Couple families with at least one child under 18 years	320,770	284,975	304,165	11.7	10.5	11.2
Couple families whose children are all 18 years and over	27,325	37,085	50,510	5.5	5.2	5.8
Lone-parent families with at least one child under 18 years	197,980	247,015	277,970	55.3	53.5	45.8
Lone-parent families whose children are all 18 years and over	37,520	45,095	67,875	19.5	16.7	16.5

1. Census families living below the low-income cut-offs (see the explanation in the methodology).
2. Families living in single-family households with no additional persons, e.g., grandparents, uncles and aunts
Source: Statistics Canada Census 2001

Figure 1: Change in average income, by income deciles, census families, Canada, 1990-2000

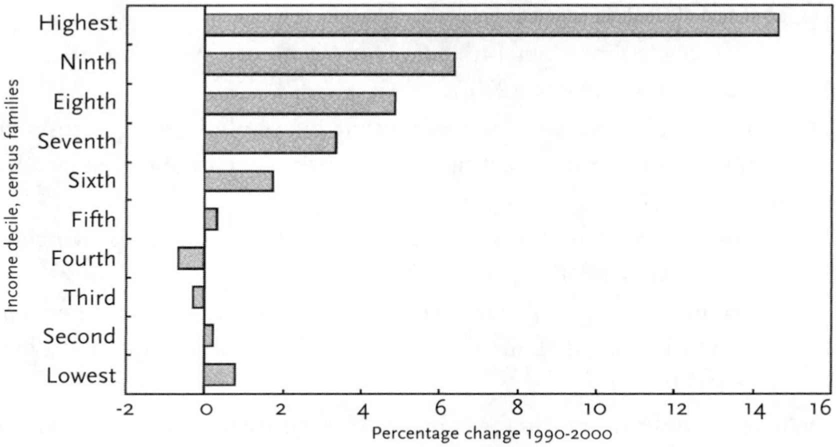

Source: Statistics Canada, Census 2001

We also know that, in the decade of the 1990s, income distribution was extremely polarized, with the top decile of families scooping up 28% of the income pie and the bottom decile pulling in only 2%. At the same time, the income gains went largely to the top deciles. As this chart from Statistics Canada shows, the top deciles of families, especially the first decile, made major gains (14% in real income for the 1st tenth of families) while the bottom 50% of families made little or no gains, and many even fell back over this period.

The Martin legacy

The overall deficit reduction strategy pushed by Paul Martin, when at the same time combined with massive personal and corporate tax cuts, left the federal government and – through a reduction in transfers – the provincial and municipal governments much less capable of dealing with social problems than in the past.

1. THE END OF THE CANADA ASSISTANCE PLAN

Not only was there a reduction in funds transferred to the provinces, but, with the abolition of the Canada Assistance Plan in 1996 and the establishment of the Canada Health and Social Transfer, the provinces were also freed from all levels of accountability, transparency, and standards or conditions in the funding and operation of social programs.

The CAP (1966) had established five basic conditions for social welfare spending:

- provide assistance to every person in need – regardless of the cause of need (CAP s.6(2)(a);
- take into account a person's basic requirements in setting social assistance rates (CAP s.6(2)(b);
- provide an appeal mechanism so that people have a legal right to challenge decisions affecting their entitlement to social assistance (CAP s.6(2)(e));
- ensure the right to social assistance regardless of one's province of origin (CAP s. 6(2)(d)); and
- not require that people who were in receipt of social assistance perform work against their will as a condition of receiving assistance (cap S.15(3)(A)).[1]

With the abolition of the CAP, many of the provinces seem to feel liberated from federal constraint and, over time, this lack of any conditions on how the very large sums of federal money should be spent ($14.5 billion in cash and tax points by 2004) has led to:

- a general diminishment or stagnation in welfare rates. (Ontario rates, which were reduced by 20% in 1995 and frozen in that year, are now worth only a fraction of their former purchasing power and Canadians on welfare are now generally living below the poverty line); and
- certain provinces imposing new punitive rules which are epitomized by the recent B.C. decision to limit welfare eligibility to two years in any five year period starting April 1, 2004.

While the Canada Health Act remained to set standards for health transfers, social programs were left on their own. They were to be attacked by a series of measures from many provincial governments, seemingly anxious to scapegoat people on welfare, or, at the very least, content to see their meager allowances decrease in real purchasing power.

2. THE NATIONAL CHILD BENEFIT

Martin has touted the National Child Benefit as the hallmark social program of the previous administration and one in which he played a key role in assuring its successful implementation.

The National Child Benefit was set up in July 1998. The program added a supplement to the existing Canada Child Tax Benefit (CCTB) for low-income families with children. The goals of the NCB were impressive:

- help prevent and reduce the depth of child poverty;
- promote attachment to the labour market by ensuring that families will always be better off as a result of working; and
- reduce overlap and duplication by harmonizing program objectives and benefits and simplifying administration. *(Social Union website)*

The NCB was designed to raise the income level of low- income families by providing supplements to poor families with children. It was also designed to target families who were of the working poor rather than welfare families who in many provinces see their benefit "clawed back." It was thought that poor families needed an incentive to get off welfare to replace benefits that would have accrued to them had they stayed on welfare – to climb the "welfare wall." The reality of the Canadian situation, however, is that many of our poor children (over 32%) live in families on welfare many of whom cannot get off it simply by a modest addition of funds, when there is no universal accessible child care or little social housing, and when minimum wage rates remain at such very low levels. In fact, a recent study by the Caledon Institute showed that, when two parents with two children were working at the minimum wage together with the NCB, they were still living below the after-tax poverty line in Ontario, Alberta, and Manitoba.

This is not to deny that the NCB had an impact on helping get many low-income children out of poverty. The NCB Report from 2002 estimates that 55,000 children in 22,900 low-income families were moved out of poverty when these families were helped by an average of about $700 each. But as the table above shows, the latest Census indicates that there are still 1.2 million poor children in Canada.

The CCCSD and most anti-poverty and child welfare groups have consistently urged that not only should the clawbacks of the NCB to children on welfare be ended, but that the combined levels of the CCTB and NCB should immediately be raised to $4,400 per child to assure that the measure is really effective. With the current program topping off at $3,243 in 2007, there is still a long way to go.

3. EMPLOYMENT INSURANCE

Social policy cannot be assessed in isolation from income support programs such as Employment Insurance. During the Martin term in Finance, the EI program became a shell of its former self. The benefit rate

Family situation	Number of parents with earnings	All children %	Children in low income %
Children living in couple families	None	2.6	12.3
	One	16.2	20.8
	Both	55.9	16.6
	Total	74.8	49.7
Children living in lone-parent families	None	4.0	20.2
	One	10.4	19.2
	Total	14.4	39.4
Children living in other situations	Total	10.8	10.8
	Total	100.0	99.9

Table 3: All children and children in low income by family situation and number of parents with earnings, Canada 2000

Source: Statistics Canada, Census 2001

was reduced to 55% of insured earnings in 1994 from 57% (down from 75% in 1975). In 1996, benefit lengths were cut and the number of weeks needed to qualify increased. More money from premiums went to the government's general revenues in 2000 than went to the EI beneficiaries – $8 billion compared to $7.2 billion. The surplus of EI contributions over payments reached $44 billion. And only around 38% of the unemployed now actually receive EI, down from 74% in 1989.

4. OTHER PROGRAMS

We do not have time in this short survey to examine Martin's role around many of the other social program such as seniors' issues or the dropping of the federally regulated minimum wage and other issues such as housing are treated elsewhere. However, a brief commentary is perhaps useful around early childhood education and parental leave programs.

Early Childhood Education

In September 2000, near the end of the Martin era in Finance, the First Ministers reached an agreement on early childhood development. This agreement, reached under the Social Union, allocated $2.2 billion in federal money over five years, beginning in 2001-2002. However, the problem, as many noted at the time, was that little of this money was going into the actual expansion of child care facilities.

So, nearly three years later, in 2003 (after Martin had left Finance), the First Ministers met again to agree on a new framework for actually expanding child care. Here, while the aim of the framework was laudable, the problem was that not only was the funding limited to $900 million over five years, but that even this amount was back-end- loaded, that is, most of the funding would only appear in the later years. The amounts were far below the $10 billion needed for a fully-funded child care program.

Parental Leave

One of the most popular programs introduced when Martin was Finance Minister was the Budget 2000 parental (maternity-paternity) leave provisions which allowed mothers and fathers to take up to a year off (up from six months) with the birth of a child. For those who are eligible for these benefits, this was undoubtedly one of the best and long-overdue pieces of social policy legislation. However, certain major problems with the program remain. First of all, many mothers and fathers are not eligible for the benefits. Only those with the right number of weeks of EI-insured work can access the program. What this means is that those in precarious or contingent work, the unemployed, and the self-employed in fact are not eligible.

At the same time, for eligible low-income workers, 55% of a low wage of $20,000 or less is far from adequate to support an expanded family.

TO SUM UP, THE CHRETIEN/MARTIN RECORD ON SOCIAL policy, with some notable exceptions, was a very neglected part of the complete legislative agenda. The overall proof is in the pudding of unacceptably high sustained levels of poverty and widening inequality in Canada.

Martin has now promised to be a "social issues" Prime Minister. He has even created a new Ministry of Social Development. His track record, while in the Chrétien cabinet, shows he is capable of supporting new and potentially valuable social policy efforts, but that often, as in the case of the NCB, such initiatives failed to live up to their first promise and were largely offset by the budgetary cutbacks and the reduction of government spending and transfers.

In his new leadership role as Prime Minister, he not only has the budgetary surpluses to do more with social policy, but also the opening of the Social Transfer to help develop, together with all major stakeholders, a whole new social architecture. He has also committed to an important urban agenda which, we hope, will move beyond bricks and mortar to deal with the growing social deficit in our cities.

Another hopeful sign is Martin's commitment to deal with issues affecting Aboriginal peoples and people with disabilities. For these two groups, Martin has made special engagements to radically alter their situation. Will social policy and social development take centre stage over the next several years, if Martin wins the mandate he seeks in the next federal election? Social policy groups will not only be waiting and watching, but will also be actively working to see that such a future materializes.◖◗

Note

[1] *From* Submissions to the Committee on Economic, social and cultural rights by the Charter Committee on Poverty Issues (CCPI) November 16, 1998 To The United Nations The Committee On Economic, Social And Cultural Rights, The Review Of The Third Report Of Canada At The Committee's 19th Session (November – December, 1998).

CHAPTER 7

Paul Martin's Health Care Legacy

by Cindy Wiggins

In 1993, Paul Martin co-authored the infamous *Red Book*, a pre-election platform document containing the Liberal Party's vision for Canada. This vision rested on a fundamental belief that "government can be a force for good in society."[1] Canada's social programs were identified as providing a framework for greater equality of social conditions among Canadians. Another five years of Tory-style cutbacks were rejected as a solution to our economic problems.

Preserving Medicare was identified as a top priority. "A Liberal government will not withdraw from or abandon the health care field... Liberals cannot and will not accept a health care system that offers a higher quality of care for the rich than for the poor."[2]

The question is: "Did Paul Martin deliver on this vision during his years as Minister of Finance?"

In his first budget as Finance Minister in 1994, the message had changed radically. "Governments," said Paul, "have been promising more than they can deliver, and delivering more than they can afford. It has to end. We are ending it."[3] One might have asked, "Who are you and what have you done with Paul?"

The freeze on transfers to the provinces for health, education, and social assistance put in place by the Mulroney government was extended, representing a cut of $1.5 billion. Funds were provided for the National Forum on Health, a process to examine the future of health care. However, the vast majority of the Forum's recommendations were never acted on by the Liberal government.

In his 1995 budget, Martin embarked on a massive downsizing of government spending on programs in order to meet deficit reduction targets. Boasting that program spending as a share of the economy would be lower than *at any time since 1951*, he targeted just over $13 billion in spending cuts.[4] Cash transfers for health, education, and social assistance were lumped into a new block fund, the *Canada Health and Social Transfer*. Combining the cuts in his first two budgets, spending on the three programs was cut by $10.6 billion over the period 1994-95 to 1997-98.[5]

Martin's creation of the CHST eliminated transparency in federal funding levels for health, education, and social assistance, making it virtually impossible to determine the level of federal support in each of the CHST program areas. At the policy level, the CHST weakened national standards in social policy, allowing provincial and territorial governments greater flexibility in the way federal dollars are spent. Effectively, Martin's creation of the CHST sparked a withdrawal of federal responsibility for – and leadership in – key national social programs. Because social programs, and social policy broadly, are a critical means of achieving equality and redressing women's economic disadvantage, Martin's 1995 budget began to dismantle the framework for social and economic equality rather than to support or expand it.

The 1996 budget froze funding for health at the same level established the previous year until 1999-2000. In 1997, $300 million was allocated towards pilot projects for a Health Transition Fund, a Canadian Health Information System, the Community Action Program for Children, and the Canada Pre-natal Nutrition Program. Between 1990 and 1997, public spending on health care declined by 0.6% per year, on average, while private spending grew by 2.2% per year, precipitated in large part by the Martin cuts.

By 1998, the fallout from the federal withdrawal from funding Medicare was clear. The federal share of provincial health spending had fallen to just over 10%, down from 50% when Medicare was first established in the 1960s. Provincial governments began moving forward with serious efforts to de-list publicly-insured health services. Some were preparing to turn over parts of the public system to the for-profit health care industry. Provincial premiers put the federal government on notice that the federal share of health dollars no longer warranted federal influence. They began a campaign to limit the federal government's enforcement of the *Canada*

Health Act. The Canadian public was increasingly voicing concern over the future of Medicare.

The 1998 Martin budget responded to one of the recommendations of the National Forum on Health by increasing the cash floor for transfers to the provinces for health, education, and social assistance from $11 billion to $12.5 billion. This paltry increase in funding failed to mitigate to any degree the impact of the previous spending cuts. By 1999, the share of private spending on health care had increased from 27.9% of the total health care spending pie to 30.4%. The public share had fallen to 69.6%, down from 75% in 1989.[6] Out-of-pocket spending on health care had grown to $14.2 billion, double what it had been just a decade ago.[7] Privatization in health care continued to grow.

Paul Martin's sixth budget in 1999 began to restore some of the cuts made in previous budgets. A one-time supplement of $3.5 billion from the previous year's surplus was added to the CHST, along with an additional $8 billion spread over a five-year period. Even though the CHST also funded post-secondary education and social assistance, the increases were defined as health care dollars.[8]

In his first budget as Finance Minister in 1994, the message changed radically. "Governments," said Paul, "have been promising more than they can deliver, and delivering more than they can afford. It has to end. We are ending it." One might have asked, "Who are you and what have you done with Paul?"

The 2000 budget allocated an additional one-time supplement of $2.5 billion over three years for all three programs. In September of that year, an agreement on increased health funding was reached between the Prime Minister and the provincial/territorial leaders. This agreement was reflected in Martin's last budget in 2001 with the allocation of $21 billion in cash transfers over five years. In addition, $2.3 billion was allocated for a Medical Equipment Fund to help provinces purchase needed medical technology. Unfortunately, the policy of handing over federal dollars to provinces without real strings attached resulted in misuse and abuse of monies in the Medical Equipment Fund.

The funding increases between 1999 and 2001 constituted a new budgeting technique which could be called "bonus budgeting." Traditionally, when new money was added to a program in a budget, this amount plus the previous total became the new funding base, or floor. Increases in subsequent years would be added to that floor, creating a new floor. In bonus budgeting, the original funding floor does not change. Any additional spending in subsequent years is added to the original floor. Thus, real growth in spending year over year is nil or minimal.

For example, in 1999, the CHST cash floor was $12.5 billion. Two billion dollars of the one-time $3.5 billion supplement was added, increasing the cash transfer to $14.5 billion for that year. In the year 2000, the cash floor reverted back to $12.5 billion. A second instalment of $1 billion from the supplement was added, as well as the first billion dollars of the $8 billion dollar increase announced in the 1999 budget. This $2 billion was added to the original cash floor of $12.5 billion, bringing the total cash transfer for 2000 back to the same $14.5 billion dollar level of the previous year. There was no real increase in spending from year to year.

Take wage increases as an example of bonus budgeting. Let's say you earn $20,000 a year. Your employer gives you a 5% raise. Your wages rise to $21,000. The next year, your employer gives you another 5% raise. You'd expect an additional $1,050 on top of your $21,000. If your employer was Paul Martin, however, your second 5% wage increase would be based on your original $20,000 wage level. You'd still be earning $21,000 even though your employer claimed you'd received a 5% increase.

This budgeting technique appears to be a permanent Paul Martin legacy. It was used in the 2003 federal budget, which implemented the financial agreement between the provinces and territories and the federal government stemming from the recommendations of the Romanow Commission. A cash floor for health funding has been set. Each year for five years, additional monies from the Health Reform Fund are added to the base. Once the HRF commitments are finished, the original base remains.

VARIOUS BUDGET SPEECHES LEAVE THE STRONG IMPRESSION that Paul Martin believes in a reduced role for government in terms of social responsibility. Rather than viewing economic and social policy as integral to each other, and critical to the economic well-being of Canadians, his view during his early years as Finance Minister was that social programs are expendable, especially when narrow fiscal goals were identified as a priority. Reducing the deficit, "come hell or high water," did leave Canada's treasured Medicare system treading dangerous waters. A Minister of Finance truly concerned about Medicare would have allocated every available surplus dollar to shore up the heavily burdened program rather than dumping those surplus dollars into debt payments to impress the IMF, the World Bank, and the OECD.

While significant public dollars were eventually restored to health care under Martin's reign, the bonus-budgeting approach signalled a short-term commitment rather than a long-term one in which the federal government plays a key leadership role in preserving and expanding Medicare. Under his watch as Finance Minister, for-profit health care took root in many provinces. Neither Martin nor the federal government as a whole took a stand on this issue, even though the encroachment of for-profit care threatens the viability of Medicare, and will inevitably result in the very situation Martin's *Red Book* guaranteed against – *a health care system that offers a higher quality of care for the rich than for the poor.*

Reducing the deficit "come hell or high water" left Canada's Medicare system treading dangerous waters. A Minister of Finance truly concerned about Medicare would have allocated every available surplus dollar to shore up the heavily burdened program.

As Prime Minister, Paul Martin appears to be trying to re-cast himself as a man with a social conscience and a deep social commitment. The depth of those musings, however, remain to be seen.

Notes

[1] *Creating Opportunity, the Liberal Plan for Canada*, September 1993, p. 10.

[2] Ibid., p. 77.

[3] The Budget Speech, February 22, 1994, p. 2.

[4] The Budget Speech, February 27, 1995, p. 4.

[5] *Budget Plan*, February, February 17, 1995, p. 51.

[6] *National Health Expenditure Trends*, 1975-1999, p. 95.

[7] *National Health Expenditure Trends*, 1975-2001, p. 18.

[8] *The Budget Plan 1999*, p. 84.

PARKS CANADA

One of the elements of a biodiversity strategy that would allow Canada to fulfill its obligations under the Convention on Biological Diversity was establishing a comprehensive parks system. Again, Paul Martin's cuts did not allow his own promises – and Canada's international commitments – to be met. Parks Canada suffered budget cuts of 40% between 1994-95 and 1998-99.[27]

The result was that the modest federal parks system proposed by the Liberal Red Book has still not been completed.[28] A lack of resources also meant a failure to adequately manage existing parks,[29] such that 30% of the total protected area is suffering "significant to severe ecological stress."[30] New parks funding was not allocated until Martin left the Finance post.

DEPARTMENT OF FISHERIES AND OCEANS:

The Department of Fisheries and Oceans (DFO) is largely an economic agency, but, as protector of Canada's fisheries resources, it retains significant responsibilities with respect to enforcing the Fisheries Act and undertaking scientific research on the state of fish stocks. Paul Martin's funding cuts – a one-third budget cut and a 40% reduction in staff[31] – have allowed the agency to do neither.

With diminishing resources brought on by the program review, Fisheries Minister Brian Tobin actually pushed to get the DFO out of freshwater fisheries.[32] Meanwhile, the number of DFO assessments of projects affecting fish habitats dropped from 12,000 in 1991-92 to 233 in 1995-96.[33] Allowing so many projects to by-pass the environmental assessment process did save time and money, but no doubt meant more environmentally dubious projects slipping through without scrutiny.

The department's scientific capacity also suffered. The world-renowned Great Lakes Laboratory for Fish and Aquatic Sciences experienced program cuts ranging from 40% to 70%.[34]

The Auditor-General stated that the DFO "had limited knowledge of stocks and habitat to determine conservation requirements and catch limits."[35]

More recently, the DFO has tried to become more "conservation-based" and adopt "a more precautionary, ecosystem-based approach," but it has rightly been pointed out that it takes greater resources, not fewer, to accomplish this.[36]

OFFLOADING RESPONSIBILITIES

The Canadian Council of Ministers of the Environment (CCME) was created in 1988 as a partnership between the 13 federal, provincial, and territorial ministers. Although its initial mandate was much broader, by 1993 the CCME's first priority was harmonizing provincial and federal environment programs to eliminate duplication and increase efficiency.[37] This process was concluded in January 1998, with all but Quebec signing the Accord on Environmental Harmonization.

Though a laudable goal, there is significant evidence that "harmonization" became nothing but a cost-saving exercise for federal environmental agencies reeling from the Martin cuts. First, a report by Parliament's Standing Committee on the Environment and other reports prepared for the CCME and the Alberta government failed to show any overlap in environmental protection or anticipated cost savings from harmonization.[38] Second, many provinces were already lacking resources and experience[39] and certain provinces – including Ontario, Quebec, and Alberta – were downsizing their environmental departments while the Accord was being negotiated.[40]

The rationale for harmonization was so flawed that, at the last minute, Environment Minister Sheila Copps balked at signing the agreement.[41] It took three years of federal cuts, and a more-compliant Environment Minister in the person of Sergio Marchi, for the Accord to finally get inked.

THE VOLUNTARY APPROACH

It is clear that the federal capacity to monitor and enforce environmental regulations eroded considerably during the Liberals' first mandate, despite Martin's promise to use environmental regulations to make Canadian businesses more competitive. There was, however, another broad policy tool that Paul Martin could have used to move towards sustainability: ecological fiscal reform. The use of fiscal incentives and disincentives, such as pollution taxes and green subsidies, to integrate environmental and economic goals, would have put less strain on federal resources. It may, in fact, have augmented them. But, despite advocating them in the Red Book,[42] and the strong endorsement of ecological fiscal reform by Martin's own Technical Committee on Business Taxation,[43] Martin almost never relied on such measures.[44]

Agencies such as Environment Canada, Natural Resources Canada (NRCan), and the DFO, facing "decreasing federal resources," had to rely instead upon voluntary measures.[45] NRCan developed a significant number of voluntary programs, in energy efficient building design and vehicle fuel efficiency, for example, but only two had any targets attached.[46] Environment Canada's voluntary programs on the release of toxic chemicals lacked effective accountability, reporting, and monitoring.[47] The two agencies collaborated on the hugely unsuccessful Voluntary Challenge and Registry program, Canada's post-Rio climate change plan. Meanwhile, by 1997 the DFO was moving towards "more self-regulation of the fisheries [by] those who benefit directly from them."[48]

THE COST OF LOOKING FOR COST SAVINGS

One-third of the budgets of natural resource-based programs were lost to the Martin cuts.[49] The $2 billion savings may have helped to balance the books, they but left a dubious environmental legacy.

Martin refused to implement a carbon tax that would discourage the use of fossil fuels. (He also failed to implement other environmental taxes and levies he once proposed.) Greenhouse gas emissions continued to climb even after the country decided to move from a voluntary program to an international agreement – the Kyoto Protocol. Even more baffling, the Finance Minister eschewed a domestic emissions trading program to meet Kyoto commitments, a program widely recognized to be the most cost-effective policy tool to reduce emissions.

The federal capacity to monitor and enforce environmental regulations eroded considerably during the Liberals' first mandate, despite Martin's promise to use environmental regulations to make Canadian businesses more competitive.

Because of Martin's inaction, Canadian businesses now have a greater fiscal incentive to break Canada's environmental laws. The Income Tax Act never specifically precluded businesses writing off fines or penalties, and so, in 1999, the Supreme Court ruled that businesses could.[50] The Court also invited Parliament to close the loophole. As Finance Minister, that would be Martin's job. But the loophole still exists, and the federal government is now forgoing hundreds of millions of dollars in corporate income taxes while giving corporate polluters less of a reason to conform to the country's laws.[51]

International commitments, like the Basel Convention, were also neglected. The Auditor-General concluded in 1997 that Environment

Canada, due to a lack of resources, had little chance of detecting illegal traffic in hazardous waste at the border, and even lower odds of doing so at marine ports and rail yards.[52]

Voluntary programs – on energy efficiency, pollution, and smog – were likewise ineffective. Canada remains one of the most energy-intensive countries on both a per capita and a GDP basis.[53] For example, per capita energy consumption of Canadians ranks 27th out of 29 OECD countries.[54] Voluntary plans for regulating toxins, like the Accelerated Reduction/ Elimination of Toxins, have faltered.[55] And smog alerts in our cities have increased since the voluntary federal-provincial agreement in 1990.[56]

Quite possibly, the cost savings of relying on band-aid solutions are illusory. Martin never did find financial solutions to clean up contaminated sites, and the escalating cost – the unfunded liability – of this task is now in the billions.[57] Also estimated in the billions are the costs of inadequate action on protecting fish stocks, reducing greenhouse gas emissions, poor air and water quality, protecting biodiversity, and the management of toxic chemicals.[58]

Worse, devolution to the provinces on environmental matters has made it much more difficult to develop a national environmental strategy on just about every issue. An endangered species act, finally passed in 2002, limited the legislation to federal land only. Alberta and British Columbia opposed ratifying Kyoto. Implementing it will likely be no easier for the new Prime Minister. The Canadian Environmental Protection Act, important legislation to manage toxic chemicals, has also "raised provincial hackles."[59]

While it would be unfair to lay the dismal Liberal record entirely at the feet of Paul Martin, the long-standing Finance Minister did play a prominent role in the dismantling of environmental protections. The year Martin left the Finance portfolio, Canada's environment Commissioner found that the federal government was not investing enough of its financial resources to fulfill its environmental commitments.[60] An assessment of the Liberal environmental record concluded that the lack of environmental leadership was caused by "Canada's ongoing unity crisis, the drive to put the government fiscal house in order, and government's push (at all levels) to create jobs through trade liberalization."[61] The latter two root causes have Martin's fingerprints all over them, while the unity crisis can be at least partly blamed on the devolution of responsibility – both social *and* environmental – to the provinces at the same time that Martin was cutting transfer payments.

Not All Bad News

Paul Martin's record on environmental issues could have been worse. For example, when each federal department was compelled to undertake a program review, Martin permitted Environment Canada to include within the calculation of its total budget the funds committed by the Conservatives under the Green Plan. Had he not done that, the department's budget would have been cut deeper, by 50% instead of 32%.[62]

There were real accomplishments, too. During the period 1997 to 2002, Martin committed $1.7 billion for federal initiatives in support of climate change.[63] The commitment, as promised in the original Red Book, included support for municipalities' green infrastructure projects ($250 million in all) in areas such as water conservation, waste management, and urban transit.[64] These initiatives did not originate with Environment Canada, but came directly from Martin himself.[65] (The funding increase to Environment Canada should be put into context; it still took Finance Minister John Manley's "greenest budget in Canadian history" just to get departmental funding back to the level it was at when the Liberals took over.[66])

> While it would be unfair to lay the dismal Liberal record entirely at the feet of Paul Martin, the long-standing Finance Minister did play a prominent role in the dismantling of environmental protections.

Other Martin promises, like cutting fossil fuel industry subsidies, were also realized. From 1993-94 to 1998-99, subsidies to non-renewable energy were cut by about two-thirds.[67] However, the nuclear industry was spared the axe. Despite Martin's promise in his 1996 budget to cap the Atomic Energy of Canada Ltd. subsidies at $100 million per year, the commitment was never met. In the 2001 budget, the nuclear industry received $211 million, an amount greater than in 1996.[68]

Meanwhile, support for renewable energy and energy efficiency grew modestly. As part of the $1.7 billion climate change commitment, a $260 million 15-year program to subsidize wind projects was announced in the 2001 budget.[69] Support for non-renewable energy projects is still greater – $200 million in 1999 vs. $12 million for renewables[70] – but the gap is closing and subsidies *per unit of production* are now higher for renewables.

During Martin's tenure, two other significant environmental achievements were delivered. On the tenth anniversary of the signing of the

Montreal Protocol, it was determined that Canada had met its obligations to reduce ozone-depleting substances in every year.[71] And, in 1996, Martin's Red Book promise to create a Commissioner of the Environment and Sustainable Development was fulfilled. The work of the independent commissioner has been invaluable in assessing the performance of this government on environmental matters. The commissioner's assessment of the Liberal record in her last report, *The Gap between Commitments and Action*,[72] must have sounded eerily familiar to Martin.

The Crystal Ball

Not surprisingly, Paul Martin held his cards much closer to his chest in last year's Liberal leadership campaign, compared to his wide-ranging environmental promises of a decade earlier. In a speech to the Montreal Board of Trade, he did suggest that a portion of the proceeds from the sale of federal shares in Petro-Canada be used to establish a Kyoto fund, but mostly he has made only vague references to economic opportunities for Canadian environmental companies.[73]

So what are we to expect from the new Prime Minister on environmental matters? Some political pundits – Edward Greenspon, Robert Chodos, and Michael Bliss, for example – have portrayed him as a reluctant deficit cutter, a pragmatist who did what he felt he had to do, given the situation he faced.[74] Increased program spending – including on the environment – is what we're told to expect. Prominent environmentalists such as Elizabeth May and David Boyd have expressed cautious optimism on Martin's environmental potential,[75] no doubt based on his sound knowledge of environmental issues and his association with Maurice Strong. The chair of the Rio Summit, Strong has said that he will act as an informal advisor to Canada's new PM.[76]

There certainly are reasons to believe that Martin will take some positive steps on the environment. He understands and believes in ecological fiscal reform, so he may move boldly on ecological taxes and tax-shifting in areas of federal jurisdiction, like toxic chemicals and carbon dioxide. And his recent funding of climate change initiatives – and qualified support for Kyoto in the Speech from the Throne – bode reasonably well for that international agreement, though Martin will have to act without alienating the provinces.

In the end, though, one has to have greater regard for a person's actions than his words when predicting future decisions. Paul Martin reneged on critical environmental, social, and free trade commitments. Most importantly, after Martin eliminated the federal deficit, he failed to honour his commitment to spend more on social and environmental programs. He dedicated only 10% of the surpluses to program spending – with the rest going to tax cuts and debt reduction – when the Liberals had promised an even split.[77] And influence and power over Martin as PM will, if anything, be even more concentrated in the hands of those who will push Martin away from decisive environmental action.

Furthermore, it is doubtful whether Martin's cabinet will include many with a genuine commitment to sustainable development. That David Anderson is still the Environment Minister is hopeful, but even if Anderson retains that portfolio, he will have a diminished supporting cast. Federal Liberals who have environmental convictions – Karen Kraft Sloan, Charles Caccia, and Clifford Lincoln for example – are unlikely to play a role, since they are either not running in the next election or have not been chosen by the new PM.[78]

The bottom line is that those who care about environmental issues can hold out some hope that Paul Martin will become the knowledgeable and enthusiastic environmentalist he always claimed to be. But they should also expect him to continue to be the political opportunist he always was.◥

Notes

[1] Chodos, Robert, Rae Murphy, and Eric Hamovitch. (1998). *Paul Martin: A Political Biography*, Toronto, James Lorimer & Co. Ltd. p. 82.

[2] Liberal Party of Canada. (1993). *Creating Opportunity: The Liberal Plan for Canada*, Ottawa. p. 64.

3 Jaimet, Kate. (2003). "The green side of Paul Martin," *The Ottawa Citizen*, (November 9), Ottawa.

4 Ibid.

5 Liberal Party of Canada. (1993). *Creating Opportunity: The Liberal Plan for Canada*, Ottawa. p. 67.

6 Boyd, David R. (2003). *Unnatural Law: Rethinking Canadian Environmental Law and Policy*, Vancouver, UBC Press. p. 231.

7 Liberal Party of Canada. (1993). *Creating Opportunity: The Liberal Plan for Canada*, Ottawa. p. 70 and p. 67.

8 Ibid. p. 67 and p. 70.

9 Lautens, Trevor. (2002). "Chretien and Martin: A Shakespearean tragedy," *Winnipeg Free Press*, (June 9), Winnipeg.

10 Toner, Glen. (1994). "The Green Plan: From Great Expectations to Eco-Backtracking…to Revitalization?" In Susan D. Phillips (ed.) *How Ottawa Spends 1994-95*, Ottawa, Carleton University Press. p. 247.

11 Stefanik, Lorna and Kathleen Wells. (1998). "Staying the Course or Saving Face?: Federal Environmental Policy Post-Rio," In Leslie A. Pal (ed.) *How Ottawa Spends 1998-99*, Toronto, Oxford University Press. p. 251.

12 Ibid. p. 252.

13 Boyd, David R. (2003). *Unnatural Law: Rethinking Canadian Environmental Law and Policy*, Vancouver, UBC Press. p. 239.

14 Smith, Douglas A. (1990). "The Agenda for Environmental Protection," In Katherine A. Graham (ed.). *How Ottawa Spends 1990-1991*, Ottawa, Carleton University Press. p. 117.

15 Environment Canada. (2000). *Environment Canada 1999-2000 Estimates*, Ottawa; and Department of Finance Canada. (2001). *Fiscal Reference Tables – September 2001*, Electronic database accessed on November 6, 2003 at http://www.fin.gov.ca/frt/2001/frt01_2e.html#Table%207

16 Boyd, David R. (2003). *Unnatural Law: Rethinking Canadian Environmental Law and Policy*, Vancouver, UBC Press. p. 240.

17 Toner, Glen. (1996). "Environment Canada's Continuing Roller Coaster Ride," In Gene Swimmer (ed.) *How Ottawa Spends 1996-97*, Ottawa, Carleton University Press. p. 100.

18 Dobbin, Murray. (2003). *Paul Martin: CEO for Canada?* Toronto, James Lorimer & Co. Ltd. p. 104.

19 Auditor General of Canada. (1998). *1998 Report of the Auditor General of Canada*, Ottawa. Section 2.108.

20 Toner, Glen. (1996). "Environment Canada's Continuing Roller Coaster Ride," In Gene Swimmer (ed.) *How Ottawa Spends 1996-97*, Ottawa, Carleton University Press. p. 125.

21 Boyd, David R. (2003). *Unnatural Law: Rethinking Canadian Environmental Law and Policy*, Vancouver, UBC Press. p. 239.

22 Commissioner of the Environment and Sustainable Development. (2002). *Report of the Commissioner of the Environment and Sustainable Development: The Commissioner's Perspective – 2002*, Ottawa. p. 7.

23 Auditor General of Canada. (1998). *1998 Report of the Auditor General of Canada*, Ottawa. Section 2.112.

24 Ibid. Section 28.243.

25 Toner, Glen. (1996). "Environment Canada's Continuing Roller Coaster Ride," In Gene Swimmer (ed.) *How Ottawa Spends 1996-97*, Ottawa, Carleton University Press. p. 118.

26 Ibid.

27 Boyd, David R. (2003). *Unnatural Law: Rethinking Canadian Environmental Law and Policy*, Vancouver, UBC Press. p. 239.

28 Commissioner of the Environment and Sustainable Development. (2002). *Report of the Commissioner of the Environment and Sustainable Development: The Commissioner's Perspective – 2002*, Ottawa. p. 6.

29 Auditor General of Canada. (1996). *1996 Report of the Auditor General of Canada*, Ottawa. Section 31.3.

30 Commissioner of the Environment and Sustainable Development. (2002). *Report of the Commissioner of the Environment and Sustainable Development: The Commissioner's Perspective – 2002*, Ottawa. p. 7.

31 Boyd, David R. (2003). *Unnatural Law: Rethinking Canadian Environmental Law and Policy*, Vancouver, UBC Press. p. 239.

32 Greenspon, Edward and Anthony Wilson-Smith. (1996). *Double Vision: The Inside Story of the Liberals in Power*, Toronto, Doubleday Canada Ltd. p. 284.

33 Juillet, Luc and Glen Toner. (1997). "From Great Leaps to Baby Steps: Environment and Sustainable Development Policy under the Liberals," In Gene Swimmer (ed.) *How Ottawa Spends 1997-98*, Ottawa, Carleton University Press. p. 186.

34 Boyd, David R. (2003). *Unnatural Law: Rethinking Canadian Environmental Law and Policy*, Vancouver, UBC Press. p. 239.

35 Commissioner of the Environment and Sustainable Development. (2002). *Report of the Commissioner of the Environment and Sustainable Development: The Commissioner's Perspective – 2002*, Ottawa. p. 7.

36 Clancy, Peter. (2000). "The H₂woes of the DFO," In Leslie A. Pal (ed.) *How Ottawa Spends 2000-2001*, Don Mills, Ontario, Oxford University Press. p. 246.

37 Stefanik, Lorna and Kathleen Wells. (1998). "Staying the Course or Saving Face?: Federal Environmental Policy Post-Rio," In Leslie A. Pal (ed.) *How Ottawa Spends 1998-99*, Toronto, Oxford University Press. p. 255.

38 Ibid p. 256; and Boyd, David R. (2003). *Unnatural Law: Rethinking Canadian Environmental Law and Policy*, Vancouver, UBC Press. p. 242.

39 Dobbin, Murray. (2003). *Paul Martin: CEO for Canada?* Toronto, James Lorimer & Co. Ltd. p. 105.

40 Stefanik, Lorna and Kathleen Wells. (1998). "Staying the Course or Saving Face?: Federal Environmental Policy Post-Rio," In Leslie A. Pal (ed.) *How Ottawa Spends 1998-99*, Toronto, Oxford University Press. p. 257; and Juillet, Luc and Glen Toner. (1997). "From Great Leaps to Baby Steps: Environment and Sustainable Development Policy under the Liberals," In Gene Swimmer (ed.) *How Ottawa Spends 1997-98*, Ottawa, Carleton University Press. p. 200.

41 Greenspon, Edward and Anthony Wilson-Smith. (1996). *Double Vision: The Inside Story of the Liberals in Power*, Toronto, Doubleday Canada Ltd. p. 285.

42 Liberal Party of Canada. (1993). *Creating Opportunity: The Liberal Plan for Canada*, Ottawa. p. 64.

43 Department of Finance. (1998). *Report of the Technical Committee on Business Taxation*, Ottawa. Chapter 9.

44 Auditor General of Canada. (1997). *1997 Report of the Auditor General of Canada*, Ottawa. Section 10.35.

45 Ibid.

46 Ibid. Section 10.52.

47 Commissioner of the Environment and Sustainable Development. (1998). *1998 Report of the Commissioner of the Environment and Sustainable Development*, Ottawa. Section 4.1.

48 Treasury Board of Canada. (1997). *Program Expenditure Detail: A Profile of Department Spending*, Ottawa. p. 29.

49 Treasury Board of Canada. (1998). *Program Expenditure Detail: A Profile of Department Spending*, Ottawa. p. 25; and Treasury Board of Canada. (1996). *Program Expenditure Detail: A Profile of Department Spending*, Ottawa. p. 28.

50 Supreme Court of Canada. (1999). *65302 British Columbia Ltd. v. Canada*, Electronic database accessed on November 13, 2003 at http://www.lexum.umontreal.ca/csc-scc/en/pub/1999/vol3/html/1999scr3_0804.html.

[51] Boyd, David. (2003). "Thanks to a tax loophole, corporate crime does pay," *The Globe and Mail*, (March 28). p. A17.

[52] Auditor General of Canada. (1997). *1997 Report of the Auditor General of Canada*, Ottawa. Section 4.2 and 4.5.

[53] Ibid. Section 10.23.

[54] Boyd, David R. (2001). *Canada vs. The OECD: An Environmental Comparison*, Victoria, Eco-Research Chair in Environmental Law and Policy.

[55] Stefanik, Lorna and Kathleen Wells. (1998). "Staying the Course or Saving Face?: Federal Environmental Policy Post-Rio," In Leslie A. Pal (ed.) *How Ottawa Spends 1998-99*, Toronto, Oxford University Press. p. 244.

[56] Boyd, David R. (2003). *Unnatural Law: Rethinking Canadian Environmental Law and Policy*, Vancouver, UBC Press. p. 243.

[57] Commissioner of the Environment and Sustainable Development. (2001). *2001 Report of the Commissioner of the Environment and Sustainable Development*, Ottawa. Section 2.3.

[58] Ibid. Main points #29.

[59] Juillet, Luc and Glen Toner. (1997). "From Great Leaps to Baby Steps: Environment and Sustainable Development Policy under the Liberals," In Gene Swimmer (ed.) *How Ottawa Spends 1997-98*, Ottawa, Carleton University Press. p. 199.

[60] Commissioner of the Environment and Sustainable Development. (2002). *Report of the Commissioner of the Environment and Sustainable Development: The Commissioner's Perspective – 2002*, Ottawa. p. 2-3.

[61] Stefanik, Lorna and Kathleen Wells. (1998). "Staying the Course or Saving Face?: Federal Environmental Policy Post-Rio," In Leslie A. Pal (ed.) *How Ottawa Spends 1998-99*, Toronto, Oxford University Press. p. 245.

[62] Juillet, Luc and Glen Toner. (1997). "From Great Leaps to Baby Steps: Environment and Sustainable Development Policy under the Liberals," In Gene Swimmer (ed.) *How Ottawa Spends 1997-98*, Ottawa, Carleton University Press. p. 195.

[63] Department of Finance. (2003). *The Budget Plan 2003*, Ottawa, Government of Canada. p. 150.

[64] Ibid.

[65] Dobbin, Murray. (2003). *Paul Martin: CEO for Canada?* Toronto, James Lorimer & Co. Ltd. p. 104.

[66] Boyd, David R. (2003). *Unnatural Law: Rethinking Canadian Environmental Law and Policy*, Vancouver, UBC Press. p. 240.

67 Commissioner of the Environment and Sustainable Development. (2000). *2000 Report of the Commissioner of the Environment and Sustainable Development*, Ottawa. p. 3-12.

68 Treasury Board of Canada. (1996). *Program Expenditure Detail: A Profile of Department Spending*, Ottawa. p. 28.

69 Department of Finance. (2001). *The Budget Plan 2001*, Ottawa, Government of Canada. p. 128.

70 Commissioner of the Environment and Sustainable Development. (2000). *2000 Report of the Commissioner of the Environment and Sustainable Development*, Ottawa. p. 3-12.

71 Auditor General of Canada. (1997). *1997 Report of the Auditor General of Canada*, Ottawa. Section 27.3.

72 Commissioner of the Environment and Sustainable Development. (2003). *2003 Report of the Commissioner of the Environment and Sustainable Development*, Ottawa.

73 Martin, Paul. (2003). "Building the 21st Century Economy," Electronic database accessed on November 10, 2003 at http://www.paulmartin.ca/home/stories_e.asp?id=704.

74 Greenspon, Edward and Anthony Wilson-Smith. (1996). *Double Vision: The Inside Story of the Liberals in Power*, Toronto, Doubleday Canada Ltd; Chodos, Robert, Rae Murphy, and Eric Hamovitch. (1998). *Paul Martin: A Political Biography*, Toronto, James Lorimer & Co. Ltd.; and Taylor, Peter Shawn. (2003). "Not Exactly as Advertised," In *National Post Business*, (October), Don Mills, Ontario.

75 Taylor, Peter Shawn. (2003). "Not Exactly as Advertised," In *National Post Business*, (October), Don Mills, Ontario. p. 60; and Jaimet, Kate. (2003). "The green side of Paul Martin," *The Ottawa Citizen*, (November 9), Ottawa.

76 Taber, Jane. (2003). "Strong to play informal role as an adviser to future PM," *The Globe and Mai*, (October 29), Toronto. p. A7.

77 Canadian Centre for Policy Alternatives. (2003). *A Funny Way of Sharing: Revisiting the Liberal Government's " 50:50" Promise*, Ottawa. p. 9.

78 Isaacs, Colin. (2003). "The Era of Paul Martin is Approaching," *Gallon Environment Newsletter*, Vol. 5, No. 7. Fisherville, Ontario, Canadian Institute for Business and the Environment.

≈

CHAPTER 9

Paul Martin and
Canada-United States Relations

by Bruce Campbell

I dentifying a Paul Martin record on Canada-U.S. relations as a guide to how he will act in the coming months and years is difficult to pin down. He does not wear Jean Chrétien's record on Canada-U.S. relations in the same way that he shares the economic or fiscal record. His past international forays have been into the multilateral arena – coordinating international efforts to reform the global financial architecture, promoting debt forgiveness for the poorest countries, and co-chairing the UN task force looking at the role of the private sector in Third World development. This difficulty is compounded by the fact that Paul Martin is a politician who has, over the years, told widely divergent constituencies what they want to hear, resulting in a record rife with ambiguities and contradictions.

In trying to ascertain where Prime Minister Martin will take Canada-U.S. relations, this analysis will pursue several lines of inquiry: Where do his business colleagues want the relationship to go? What has he actually said or done about Canada-U.S. relations before becoming Prime Minister? What has he said and done so far as Prime Minister?

1. Where do Martin's business colleagues want the relationship to go?

Paul Martin is a product of the business class. This is his world, where his close friends are, and where he feels most comfortable. It should also be said that these are the same people who bankrolled his leadership bid and to whom he is therefore beholden. The big business lobby, the Canadian Council of Chief Executives (CCCE), formerly the BCNI, figures prominently as the likeliest mirror on the future. Martin himself was a member of the BCNI when he was head of Canada Steamship Lines.

After September 11, big business intensified its push for deeper integration between the two countries. The C.D. Howe Institute launched its border paper series calling for deeper integration across a range of areas, from a common resource policy (including energy) to a customs union (including common trade policy), to common security perimeter, to a common currency. The series led off with a paper by Wendy Dobson advocating another mega-negotiation with the U.S. with everything on the table, the basic trade-off being economic security (Canada) for homeland security (United States).

More recently, the Canadian Council of Chief Executives, led by Tom d'Aquino, has been pushing its *North American Security and Prosperity Initiative*. This warrants closer scrutiny since past CCCE initiatives have borne a striking resemblance to government policy.

The CCCE plan calls for action on five fronts. The first is a "reinvented border... open for business and closed to terrorism... a shared checkpoint." This North American security perimeter would involve developing "shared approaches to commercial processing, infrastructure, intelligence, and policing, a North American identity document, and a shared institution to provide oversight."

The second is harmonizing regulations – e.g., standards, inspection and certification procedures. It also involves trade remedy, access, ownership, and labour mobility issues. The third priority area is the creation of a common resource security pact that would resolve, once and for all, issues of resource pricing and subsidies that are behind current trade disputes. Fourth is the creation of a *North American Defense Alliance* to defend against missile attacks, and other threats from the air, land and sea. This implies a major increase in military spending to enhance "Canadian homeland security capacity within North America." And finally, the creation of bi-national commissions to move forward these action areas.

2. What has Paul Martin said and done prior to becoming Prime Minister?

Martin was elected to Parliament in 1988 on a liberal platform of opposition to the FTA. During his period in the opposition, he and the Liberal party were critical of NAFTA. In 1992 he called NAFTA "a lousy agreement... very damaging to the country... It should be renegotiated or scrapped." *(Toronto Star, June 28, 1992).* The Liberals came to power in 1993 on a promise articulated in the party's pre-election Red Book to re-negotiate NAFTA (the deal had not yet been implemented) or scrap it. They did neither. Martin was the co-author of the Red Book.

He also advocated a harder line on the ongoing American harassment of Canadian exports, specifically, toughening Canadian trade laws to help exporters fight back. In response to a dumping action taken against Regina-based steel producer IPSCO, Martin said, "I'm a pacifist, but when you're getting punched in the face every day, there comes a time when you have to punch back." *(Toronto Star June 23 1993).*

> The Liberals came to power in 1993 on a promise articulated in the party's pre-election Red Book to renegotiate NAFTA (the deal had not yet been implemented) or scrap it. They did neither. Martin was the co-author of the Red Book.

The opposition politician Paul Martin also wanted to take a harder line on foreign investment. Responding to the takeover of the Canadian biotechnology firm Connaught Laboratories, he said: "We must never again see this nation debate whether a Canadian company should be taken over by foreign interests or whether it should be allowed to stay a small Canadian company." *(Toronto Star Jan.30, 1990).* However, as Finance Minister, Martin raised the foreign ownership limits on banks to a point where foreign control of a Canadian bank is now possible.

In his 1990 bid for the Liberal leadership, Martin described himself as a Canadian nationalist, warning that, unless Canada staked out distinct foreign, economic and social policies, we would become an American colony. "The country has ten years in which we are going to become either a colony of the United States or, *de facto*, a political groupie of the Americans, or we are going to become an independent nation. *(Barthos, Toronto Star, Dec.18, 2003).*

More recently, Martin told biographer John Gray he believes that the approach to the United States should be pro-active and outward-looking, that the exercise of sovereignty cannot be based on protectionism. He still defines himself, according to Gray, as a Walter Gordon economic nationalist, although, if true, it would position him (as it did Gordon) way out of sync with the views of the big business community. The evidence suggests otherwise.

Martin became involved in international economic governance issues especially in the wake of the 1990s international financial crises. Although the idea originated with U.S. Treasury Secretary Lawrence Summers, Martin took a lead role in establishing the G-20, bringing in a group of "emerging economy" nations into the process of reforming the international financial architecture *(Dobbin, 2003:165)*. Extending the G-20 as a model in reforming the structures of global governance in other areas is also a priority for Martin.

On the war with Iraq, Martin was leaning to the pro-war camp. On the eve of the invasion, he told a high school audience: "I don't think there is any doubt, if there ever was... that [Saddam Hussein] has weapons of mass destruction." *(National Post, March 7, 2003)* However, after Chrétien's decision not to participate in the war, Martin did not publicly dissent from the government's position. But it is fair to ask: what choice would Paul Martin have made had he been Prime Minister at the time?

On the Bush administration's national missile defense program (NMD), Martin said, "I don't know if the missile defense system will work... the Americans are asking us if we would like to cooperate... If a missile is going over Canadian air space, I want to know. I want to be at the table before that happens... My sovereignty says you don't send missiles up over my airspace unless I'm there. *(Victoria Times Colonist, April 29, 2003.)* He was quick to assert that this program will not lead to the weaponization of space, which he opposes, though many experts say that NMD is clearly part of a U.S. agenda for the military domination of space. According to Lloyd Axworthy and Michael Byers *(Globe and Mail, November 17, 2003)*, support for NMD would constitute a sea change in Canada's policy on non-proliferation of weapons of mass destruction. It would harm Canada's reputation in the world community as a supporter of multilateralism and the rule of international law. On the other hand, and perhaps more to the point in terms of Martin's priorities, it would help to repair relations with the United States, even if support was only symbolic. Moreover, it would assure Canadian corporations access to the contracts associated with this program.

The Politics of Achievement, the document that accompanied Martin's speech to the November Liberal convention, made clear that repairing the strained relationship with the United States, beginning with common security concerns, was a key priority.

Six months earlier, in a more detailed foreign policy statement, Martin outlined four steps to strengthen the bilateral partnership: 1) more face-to-face encounters among the leadership of both countries at all levels of government and civil society; 2) a permanent cabinet committee chaired by himself, with the goal being to organize horizontally under one umbrella the many dimensions of the relationship from security to trade; 3) a Commons standing committee on Canada-U.S. relations; and 4) a *national security policy* for Canada that "would direct and coordinate military and non- military efforts. It would include internal security, intelligence, policing, the Coast Guard, and customs and emergency preparedness – all focused on protecting our country against terrorist threats that emanate from beyond our shores or within our borders." It would include such border measures as land, sea and air surveillance, but also international contributions to peace and security.

"We must never again see this nation debate whether a Canadian company should be taken over by foreign interests or whether it should be allowed to stay a small Canadian company," Martin said. As Finance Minister, he raised the foreign ownership limits on banks to a point where foreign control of a Canadian bank is now possible.

(This passage was reproduced verbatim in the *Politics of Achievement*.)

He told biographer John Gray that Canada must cooperate with the United States on defense issues to protect against international terrorism. "He stressed the word cooperation. 'I really want to cooperate with the Americans... that's really important. I don't want the Americans to think they can come in here and help us. We'll do our own thing.' For Martin, cooperation on security does not extend to immigration. 'We will have to set our own immigration policy'."

Martin has been vague, for the most part, on various deep economic integration proposals, though as Finance Minister he opposed the "common currency" (adopting the American dollar) proposal. In the wake of September 11, he called the border the biggest non-tariff barrier to trade and one that had to be given the very highest priority. Martin is very much

in the deep integration camp. His common security priorities closely parallel those of the CCCE. He will likely pursue a piecemeal approach. How
fast and how far will be determined by his ability to build a public consensus in Canada and generate interest among U.S. policy-makers.

3. What has Paul Martin, Prime Minister, said or done with regard to Canada-U.S. relations?

First, his key appointments. He appointed Peter Nicholson as his senior
policy advisor. Nicholson, a former vice-president at the Bank of Nova
Scotia, was Martin's senior policy advisor at Finance in the mid-1990s.
He, along with the Deputy Finance Minister at the time, David Dodge,
were the main architects of the massive program cuts of the mid-1990s.
Dodge is currently Bank of Canada governor, appointed with Martin's
blessing. Whether the rumours that Dodge will move from the Bank of
Canada to the Privy Council are true or not, he will continue to have
Martin's policy ear. Both men favour measures to integrate the two econo-
mies more deeply.

At the 1991 Aylmer conference, which reversed the Liberals' anti-FTA
stance, Nicholson was talking about adjusting to globalization, shrinking
the role of the state, overhauling social policy, and expanding free trade.
His recent writings suggest there is much more to be done on these fronts.
Dodge gave a frank speech last August at the annual Couchiching conference in which he linked security integration and economic integration,
and outlined the following desirable steps to reduce what he called "border risk" for Canada:

- a common external tariff (customs union),
- harmonization of trade and commercial policies and regulation;
- an end to trade remedies in North America; and
- a uniform policy on federal and state/provincial subsidies.

He further recommended removing barriers to trade in cultural, legal,
financial, and communications services, and extending NAFTA coverage
to agricultural products. Dodge advocated moving to a single continental
market: "To achieve maximum economic benefits, harmonization of regu-
latory standards and practices, particularly with respect to capital and labour markets, should be a priority as we move forward."(8) Monetary
union, he said, should be considered once significant progress toward a
single market is achieved.

Martin's cabinet appointments reflect his promise to deal decisively with U.S. concerns about Canada's commitment to security. He appointed David Pratt to Defense. Pratt is a hawk who criticized Chrétien's defense policy, including its decision not to support the Iraq war. He supports greatly increasing military spending, more troops, greater military integration with the U.S., and Canadian participation in the U.S. missile defense program. (Defense experts are calling for an immediate $5 billion increase.)

Martin appointed Anne McLellan Deputy Prime Minister and Minister of the new federal Department of *Public Safety and Emergency Preparedness* to embed security cooperation relations with the U.S. Department of Homeland Security. It will address terrorist threats, as well as threats from health pandemics to natural disasters (though not immigration). It is designed is convince the Americans that Canada is now serious about security issues. And he appointed former Tory and newly-minted Liberal Scott Brisson as his parliamentary point man responsible for Canada-U.S. relations.

> Martin's cabinet appointments reflect his promise to deal decisively with U.S. concerns about Canada's commitment to security.

Pratt announced in early January Canada's decision, in principle, to participate in the U.S. missile defense program, a move that was warmly received by the Bush administration. The Throne Speech reiterated his commitment to a new, "more sophisticated" relationship with the United States, to developing a national security policy, and to new border infrastructure investments.

Other security-oriented measures announced in Martin's first days in office include:

- The appointment of a "national security advisor" reporting directly to the Prime Minister, to better ensure threats and intelligence reach the Prime Minister and his inner cabinet.
- A foreign policy and defense review to define the new national security policy, chaired by Foreign Minister Bill Graham, to report in the fall.
- A cabinet committee on Canada-U.S. relations chaired by Martin himself.
- A cabinet committee on Security, Public Health and Emergencies, chaired by McLellan.
- A House of Commons national security standing committee.

Martin's first meeting with President Bush at the Americas Summit in Monterrey, Mexico, though thin on substance, produced "very, very good vibes." Martin put a brave face on his failure to gain a commitment from the U.S. to "respect the Canadian passport," calling Bush's promise to inform the Canadian government before deporting Canadian citizens to third countries "precedent-setting." Bush promised that Canadian citizens would in future have access to consular officials.

Most observers note that this would not have stopped the Arar deportation to Syria. Moreover, the U.S. is already obligated under existing international agreements to give Canadian citizens prior access to consular officials. George Bush did not rule out breaking these international obligations again if national security interests warranted. As U.S. Ambassador Celluci candidly admitted, "The United States will continue to do what it has to do, and at times act unilaterally if we believe it is in the security of the people of the United States."*(Walkom, Toronto Star Dec. 13, 2003)*. (Although the government will hold a public inquiry into the Arar case, it will not likely probe broader issues relating to the exchange of security information with U.S. officials by the RCMP.)

> Martin put a brave face on his failure to gain a commitment from the U.S. to "respect the Canadian passport," calling Bush's promise to inform the Canadian government before deporting Canadian citizens to third countries "precedent-setting."

Martin did extract a reversal from Bush on his decision to exclude Canadian companies from participating in the Iraq reconstruction contracts despite Canada's commitment of $600 million to the reconstruction effort. Canadian firms will now be able to bid on the second round of contracts. This was likely a *quid pro quo* for the Canadian support of the U.S. missile defense program. There were vague assurances of close cooperation to find continental solutions to the BSE-infected beef industry, but, not surprisingly, nothing on the intractable softwood lumber dispute.

At the Americas Summit and at the annual Davos gathering of the world's corporate and political élites in Switzerland, Martin made a case for international trade agreements going beyond liberalization to include social development provisions in areas such as health care and education. He was careful, however, not to provoke American ire by linking poverty and inequality with terrorism, as Chrétien bluntly did. Canadians who are aware of the social devastation and rampant increase in inequality caused by successive Martin budgets acknowledge that such statements should be taken with a large grain of salt.

BOTH SIDES ARE TRUMPETING THE NEW FRIENDLY TONE OF Canada-U.S. relations. This was to be expected and easy to accomplish. The real question is: how, or how far, will Paul Martin diverge substantively from the policies of his predecessor?

Martin is already moving quickly on security to show that Canada can now be trusted to take this matter seriously. This is the litmus test for Washington. It will be expecting significant increases in military spending. Martin will likely save the bulk of this spending for the 2005 budget, after the foreign policy review is completed. He will take great pains to emphasize that the *national* security agenda is not being developed to satisfy Washington, but to advance Canada's national interests.

His early priority has been to secure access for Canadian business to U.S. military contracts, both for Iraq reconstruction and for the missile defense program. This goal has been achieved.

Martin, like Tom d'Aquino, sees (anti-terrorist) security and economic issues as inseparable. Security is a precondition for ensuring the stability of the now highly integrated and vulnerable Canadian economy. Economic security and deepening the integration of the two economies will be his most important priority in the coming years.

His economic integration agenda will closely parallel that of his big business allies. The biggest difference is that he will avoid any "Big Idea" approaches. He will move step-by-step, below the radar where possible. His agenda will include harmonization of regulations, tariffs, standards, etc.; measures to enhance the cross-border movement of goods, services and people; development of common approaches to trade, resources, competition policy, subsidies, etc.

He will move carefully, given public sensitivities about becoming more closely tied to the U.S. and subservient to its interests, and about his big business connections. But Martin is accomplished in the art of persuasion, and has an effective PR team that brought Canadians on side in the war on the deficit. His "spinners" will no doubt try to replicate this success on deep integration. We can expect a campaign laced with nationalist rhetoric that will position Canada as a confident global player with nothing to fear from closer relations with the United States.

Martin will portray his policies as asserting rather than ceding sovereignty. He will try to anticipate U.S. wishes and then move first to be seen to be pro-active. [This has been described as the "finlandization" of foreign policy.] Though Martin will avoid the sycophantic Mulroney-style approach to the relationship, we should not expect the kind of policy divergence or public criticism of the late Chrétien era. There will likely be no more rocking the U.S. policy boat; no public dissent from U.S. polices comparable to Chrétien's stand on Iraq.

Paul Martin wants to make his mark on the international stage. Bolstered by his past international accomplishments, He sees Canada, and himself, strategically positioned to play the role of the catalyst and leader in creating the new multilateral architecture of the 21st century. He sees himself, perhaps naively, as the one to persuade the American hyperpower of the error of its unilateralist ways and to come round to seeing its own long-term interest in embracing multilateralism.

Everything about his record suggests that Paul Martin will seek to take the country further down the deep integration path, a fact that is hard to reconcile with his claim to being a Walter Gordon economic nationalist. Under his watch as Finance Minister, Canada's economic independence and social distinctiveness have been further compromised. Martin's assertions about protecting Canadian sovereignty should be viewed with the skepticism that comes from having witnessed the bitter social fallout from the fiscal policies of a Finance Minister who once claimed he was merely a foot soldier in his father's crusade for social justice.☙

References:

Dobbin, M. (2003) *Paul Martin: CEO for Canada?* Lorimer.

Gray, J. (2003) *Paul Martin: The Power of Ambition*, Key-Porter

Clarkson, S. and Banda, M.(2003) *Paradigm Shift or Paradigm Twist*, paper presented to a conference on deep integration, York University, October 15-16, 2003

CHAPTER 10

From J. Lo to Bono

Does Paul Martin's International Development Agenda Hit the Right Note?

by Joe Gunn

"(Paul Martin's) *still not a household word abroad. But among those who know how politics works, he is the man to become the star. He is Jennifer Lopez three years ago.*"[1]

P aul Martin's commitment to make his mark on international development issues was evident when, in the midst of the Liberal leadership campaign, he accepted a request to co-chair the United Nations Development Program's Commission on the Private Sector and Development. The Commission is comprised of conservative but powerful personalities such as Ernesto Zedillo, former President of Mexico, Robert Rubin, former U.S. Treasury Secretary, Carleton Fiorina, chair and CEO of Hewlett Packard, and economist Hernando de Soto, president of the Lima-based Institute for Liberty and Democracy, among others. It is charged with finding ways to encourage the domestic private sector of poor nations to provide an impetus for development. But even in this context is it fair to compare Paul Martin (as one of the Commissioners actually did) to the lithe pop music and movie star Jennifer Lopez? Even though her erstwhile beau, Ben Affleck, bought her everything from a Rolls-Royce to a gem-encrusted toilet seat, hasn't her career been much more focused on form than substance?

Canadian Liberals are betting on another, perhaps less evocative, comparison. When rock superstar Bono, lead singer of U-2, agreed to take the stage at the mid-November 2003 Liberal Party Convention, it was at Martin's invitation. The two first met in 2000 to discuss their mutual concern to provide debt relief for poor countries. Bono has maintained an active passion for development, and more recently advocated urgent action to change patent laws to allow the provision of cheaper generic drugs to African states confronting the HIV/AIDS pandemic. He has used his celebrity status to garner opportunities to encounter world leaders, recount his own experiences of the ravages of underdevelopment, and impress upon them the need for change. As Bono stated at the 2002 World Economic Forum, "The great thing about hanging out with Republicans is that it's very unhip for both of us. There's a parity of pain here."

As a politician, long before he became Prime Minister, Paul Martin worked steadfastly to develop an international profile as a statesman sensitive to the needs of poor countries. In 1999, Martin was named the inaugural chairman of the Finance Ministers' G-20, an organization made up of the G-7 wealthy countries but, for the first time, including emerging market nations. Martin wanted to enable a broader discussion on international economic issues, especially after the disastrous handling of the Asian economic crisis of 1997. Based on this positive dialogue, in October 2003 he called for a Leaders' G-20 meeting to discuss similar themes. Admired for his penchant for consultation with a wide variety of Canadians, including civil society organizations, in 1999 Martin signed the Jubilee debt petition at the back of his church. He also joined 164 members of Parliament who voted in favour of a motion that the government of Canada enact a tax on international financial transactions designed to slow the flow of "hot money." [2]

Martin set out his vision for Canadian foreign policy in an April 2003 speech, and elaborated subsequently upon the main points during his leadership campaign. He has consistently called for a substantial foreign and defence policy review. His engagement with international development issues seems substantive, and real.

So, while spurious comparisons to pop figures of the day may provide the occasional smile, they guarantee little analytical depth. The same might be said, certainly, for political speeches or even campaign promises. Perhaps the most concrete indication of Martin's future resolve on international economic matters can be gleaned from taking a sober look at his actual past practice as Finance Minister in two particularly indicative areas: international development financing, and international debt relief for the poorest countries.

The Martin Record on International Development Assistance

>"I think poverty is a moral issue, and I think that certainly, in terms of Canadians, our values are such that we regard it as a moral issue. Long before the fight against terrorism... the worldwide target of 0.7% of GNP [has been] a means of judging whether a country is doing what it ought to be doing or not, and most of us unfortunately are not. . ."[3]

In mid-2003, UN Secretary-General Kofi Annan was considering whom he might appoint as co-chairs of the Commission on the Private Sector and Development. One choice would necessarily be former Mexican President (currently a director of the Yale Center for the Study of Globalization) Ernesto Zedillo. After all, Zedillo had played a major role in the preparation of the UN's Financing for Development Report, as well as the international conference of the same name that took place in Monterey, Mexico. From that meeting, the international community recognized that an additional US$50 billion per annum would need to be committed if world leaders were to keep their promise to meet the Millennium Development Goals by the year 2015.[4] Surely, to meet the challenge of providing these funds, Annan would have wanted to enlist the support of a political leader from the wealthy North who had put real money behind international development programs designed to assist the most needy.

But other considerations were also at play. One of Annan's closest confidants is Maurice Strong, former president of Power Corporation, and the mentor who gave Paul Martin his start in business. According to journalist Marci MacDonald, it was Strong who arranged Martin's appointment as co-chair of the Commission. "Strong admits he hoped to leaven the former Finance Minister's reputation as a flinty deficit-slayer with the righteous lustre of a Third World champion." Mr. Strong said, "People think of him (Paul Martin) as a very tough Finance Minister who made some very tough decisions. But now they'll see the other side of him. He's driven genuinely by a desire to do something useful for society."[5]

Countries of the global South are anxious to see evidence of this "other side" because it was Martin who, as Finance Minister, imposed the deepest cuts to overseas development assistance in the modern history of Canada's aid program.

In 1992, before the Liberals under Jean Chrétien came to power, Martin had an important role to play in the preparation of the famous party platform now referred to simply as "*The Red Book*." In this document, the Liberal party once again committed itself to reach the elusive goal (proposed initially by Lester Pearson) of spending 0.7% of Gross National Product (GNP) on development assistance. Yet, one year later, when Martin was appointed to the Finance portfolio, he did not deliver on this promise. Instead, with only the exception of his final year as Finance Minister, he allowed Canada's overseas development assistance budget, as a percentage of GNP, to *fall* in every year in which he held the reins of economic power.[6]

Paul Martin's infamous budget of February 1995 was where the real damage began, leading one seasoned development worker to refer to it as "a terrorist attack on the aid budget." In one fell swoop, 15% of the foreign aid program was swept away. Unfortunately, however, the NGO sector took a disproportionate share of the cut. Organizations that might have been critical of Canadian policies, and those that educated a constituency looking for real solutions to world poverty, were targeted. Development education "learner centres" were among the 90 groups that suffered cuts of 100% of their Canadian International Development Agency (CIDA) funding, resulting in the closure of almost all of these community-based groups.

For example, the Global Education Program, a fund administered by Canadian teachers' unions to develop curriculum materials on international issues for use in schools, was eliminated. Provincial coordinating councils of NGOs were also gutted, contributing to a situation where the overwhelming majority of Canadian development NGOs became concentrated in Toronto, Montreal, or Ottawa. The Canadian Council for International Cooperation (CCIC), the umbrella group of (then 115, but today less than 100) voluntary organizations working for development in the global South and Canada, responded with this statement: "By cutting funds to NGOs, CIDA is also hobbling its most cost-efficient mechanism for delivering the programs it deems most vital – primary health care, clean drinking water, sanitation, and nutrition and family planning programs."[7]

Throughout the decade, the damage continued. It should be astounding to many Canadians to realize that, even without accounting for changes in the real value of the currency, Canada invested more money in overseas development assistance in 1991-92 (a decade ago and under a Conservative government!) than *any* Paul Martin budget ever provided.

Of course, Canada was not the only country that was cutting development assistance budgets during the 1990s. But why did Paul Martin decide to make the Canadian cuts so much more severe than others? And why, after the deficit was defeated, was aid spending not prioritized? In comparison with 21 OECD donors, only Belgium, Italy, Finland, and the United States cut more deeply than Canada.[8] Whereas the average ratio of development assistance spending to GNP of the wealthy countries stayed around 0.4%, the Canadian downward plunge to 0.27% and even 0.25% was much more severe.[9]

> Paul Martin's infamous budget of February 1995 was where the real damage began, leading one seasoned development worker to refer to it as "a terrorist attack on the aid budget."

Martin's cuts to development assistance were overly damaging, even when compared to other sectors hard-hit by his deficit-trimming efforts. For example, again using the years 1990-91 to 2000-01 and measuring in real 1999 dollars, the development assistance budget was devastated by a 31.9% cut, compared to overall cuts to program spending of 6.54% and of 15.07% specifically to Defence.[10] Based on such realities, it becomes difficult to square Martin's oft-stated commitment to international development with his decision as Finance Minister to consistently demand such inordinately large cuts from the aid budget.

A dozen leaders of Canadian civil society organizations emerged cautiously optimistic after a September 30, 2003 meeting with Martin in which his role in the UN Commission on the Private Sector and Development was discussed. Development practitioners understand that beyond the issue of the *volume* of Canadian aid is the more crucial question of the *nature* of such spending. NGOs have consistently urged that Canadian development assistance should be directed towards alleviating poverty, rather than tying aid to purchases of Canadian goods and services or promoting Canadian business abroad. Field experience shows that private sector investment is neither a replacement for aid nor for public investment in areas like health care and education. It will be fascinating to see Martin's mark on the UN Commission's report, due in early 2004. Will the recommendations be in agreement with CIDA's September 2003 strategy for expanding opportunities through private sector development? Can the private sector eradicate poverty?

It is clear is that a Paul Martin government must play catch-up if it hopes to respect its stated commitment to meet the Millennium Development Goals. To succeed, both the amount and the nature of Canadian assistance, as well as efforts to empower the civil society organizations needed to contribute to this effort, will need to be substantially enhanced.

The Martin Record on Cancellation of the International Debts of the Poorest Countries

"This is a moratorium. This is not a forgiveness of interest payments. The ultimate debt forgiveness only arises when, in fact, (eligible countries) have completed the programs."[11]

The decade of the 1990s, following as it did upon the end of the Cold War, should have witnessed economic and social development in the countries of the global South. However, not only did wealthy Northern governments slash their aid budgets, but, more fundamentally, the global economic architecture conspired against development.

For the poorest countries of the global South, the IMF and World Bank lending policies had long been targeted as little more than new colonial structures that prevented national development. The debt crisis, while not new, had reached increasingly unsustainable proportions. For every $1 that Northern countries provided in aid, over $6 came back from less developed countries in debt servicing costs. Many countries spent more on debt servicing (seldom repayment) than they spent on health and education.[12] As the end of the second millennium drew near, NGOs in the global South and world religious leaders urgently repeated their calls for the cancellation of the international debts of the poorest countries.

The Jubilee 2000 – or Drop the Debt – Campaign eventually spread to over 40 countries. In the spring of 1997, 37 organizations led by the Christian churches formed the Canadian Ecumenical Jubilee Initiative (CEJI) and planned a three-year campaign of reflection, education and action. On September 28, 1998, the campaign was launched on Parliament Hill (to coincide with the Commonwealth Finance Ministers' meeting) and in 28 other Canadian cities and towns.[13] Around the globe, similar campaigns encouraged citizens to sign petitions calling for debt cancellation, with a view to presenting these to the leaders of the G-8 countries in Cologne, Germany, in June 1999.

Over 645,000 signatures (or one in every 50 Canadians) were eventually gathered in Canada, including one from the Finance Minister himself. This became the largest petition in Canadian history (until, that is, comedian Rick Mercer of *This Hour Has 22 Minutes* asked Canadians to sign an electronic petition to change Canadian Alliance leader Stockwell Day's first name to "Doris.") In Cologne, the international campaign presented 17 million signatures demanding debt cancellation to the leaders of the G-8.

Due to the fact that the debt issue had been a concern of Canadian churches for over two decades, and that the Canadian campaign had consciously developed and cultivated relationships with the more radical Jubilee campaigns of the global South, it demanded more profound action than did some of the European efforts. For example, CEJI called for 100% cancellation of the debt of 50 low-income countries (when the World Bank and IMF were only offering a plan to assist 35 nations.) Influenced also by the Quebec-based Jubilee campaigners, the CEJI petition forcefully opposed the structural adjustment conditionalities imposed by the World Bank and the IMF on any country eligible for debt relief.[14]

The response of Finance Minister Martin and his international counterparts in Cologne fell short. Although the G-8 announced its "Cologne Debt Initiative" with great fanfare, the plan was based on its failed 1996 predecessor, the HIPC (Highly Indebted Poor Countries) Initiative. It did not offer debt cancellation, but debt "sustainability" (i.e., supposedly increasing a country's ability to eventually pay debts back.) HIPC continued to condition debt relief on the implementation of structural adjustment measures, forcing countries to reduce social expenditures, privatize services and industries, liberalize markets, eliminate price controls and subsidies, etc. The revised HIPC proposal was too little, too slow, and did not cover enough of the countries desperately in need of debt cancellation.[15]

Over the three-year campaign, Canadian debt activists constantly maintained a focus on Finance Minister Paul Martin, and, through the efforts of the Halifax Initiative[16], personally met with him at least six times. In order to maintain public pressure, three postcard actions (in August and October 1999 and May 2000) were initiated. After Hurricane Mitch struck Central America in the autumn of 1998, and massive floods enveloped

Mozambique in the spring of 2000, special campaigns were initiated to request immediate debt moratoria for these devastated countries. In a March 1999 speech, Prime Minister Chrétien responded. Canada would propose that "the industrialized countries forgive 100% of the debt owed to them by those least developed of the HIPCs."[17] Later, the Finance Department also cancelled $900,000 in bilateral debts owed by Bangladesh, which was not an HIPC country.

Although this sounded like progress, it was translated into a concrete step forward with Martin's December 2000 announcement that Canada would extend a debt payment moratorium on bilateral debt owed to Canada by 11 countries. The genesis of this decision occurred at the August 2, 2000 meeting between Martin and debt campaigners. While Finance Department officials argued they could not act out of step with the Paris Club of lenders, CEJI suggested to Martin that it was well within his power to act on Canada's bilateral debt. "He pondered this for a moment and then asked his officials why not. They didn't have an answer. A few months later, the moratorium was announced – what amounts to cancellation but falling within Paris Club rules."[18]

While CEJI praised Martin for this initiative, the coalition recognized that "the effect will be a drop in the bucket," since Canada was owed less than one-half of one percent of impoverished country debt.[19] "A much more substantial action, as called for by the Jubilee movement," suggested a CEJI participant, "would be for the international financial organizations like the World Bank and IMF to call a moratorium on the massive debt payments that they hold. Until then, the Jubilee 2000 call will not have been heard."[20]

Nonetheless, Paul Martin's action set the standard for positive initiatives among the reluctant G-8 members. To some extent, the Canadian moratorium on bilateral debts was emulated by Britain and even Bill Clinton. Canada's position by Christmas 2000 was the most progressive among the G-8 countries, because it broke with their consensual inaction and actually suspended debt payments. Some debt campaigners reported that Martin's call for other countries to join Canada's moratorium stance "cost him" among his international peers during their September 2000 Prague meeting, and that "we must recognize what we have won."[21]

Throughout those years of engagement on debt issues, Paul Martin seemed to be a man struggling with two visions. On the one hand, he could advocate for socially progressive polices like debt relief. On the other hand, his personal predilection for market ideology would not allow for debt cancellation without adherence to stringent neo-liberal economic conditionalities imposed by the IMF and World Bank. Whatever progressive positions on international economic issues Martin took were limited by his ultimate faith in market solutions, thus limiting the impact of social and economic progress for the most vulnerable.

There may be little cause to assume that civil society organizations involved in the struggle for global economic justice will reach agreement with Prime Minister Paul Martin on fundamental issues related to the exploitative design of the international economy. His cuts to the development assistance budget over the 1990s suggest that he places scant priority there. Yet, perhaps the case study of the international debt campaign suggests that, when compelling policy proposals backed by massive public pressure are brought to bear, Martin can be engaged to take leadership on international issues.

> Whatever progressive positions on international economic issues Martin took were limited by his ultimate faith in market solutions.

No, Paul Martin shouldn't be compared to Jennifer Lopez, or even to Bono. In Bono's speech to the Liberal convention, he asked, "How will I thank Paul Martin for this invitation? I'm gonna become the biggest pain in his life." Canadians also need to ensure that Prime Minister Martin's decisions are in tune with their own aspirations for serious and long-overdue action to eradicate global poverty.❧

Joe Gunn would like to thank John Mihevc and John Dillon of KAIROS Toronto and Derek McCuish of the Social Justice Committee of Montreal for their helpful comments on earlier drafts of this chapter.

Notes

[1] Hernando d de Soto, in *The National Post*, quoted in Duncan Cameron, "Prime minister-to-be becomes UN's champion of social justice," *The CCPA Monitor*, October 2003, pg. 2.

[2] Popularly know as "the Tobin Tax" after Nobel Prize winning economist James Tobin originally proposed it, the vote in Parliament took place in March 23, 1999 and was passed with 83 votes against the NDP-sponsored motion.

[3] Paul Martin, CBC Sunday Report, November 18, 2001.

[4] In 2000, all 189 United Nations member states pledged to meet the Millennium Development Goals by 2015. These include commitments to reduce by half both the proportion of people living on less than a dollar a

day as well as those suffering from hunger, and to ensure all children have the opportunity to complete primary school, among others. See: http://www.un.org/millenniumgoals/index

[5] Marci McDonald, "Blind Trust: How much do we really know about Canada's next prime minister?" *The Walrus*, October 2003, p. 44.

[6] See: Table #1. By the time of Mr. Martin's final budget, presented in December 2001, the overseas development assistance to GNP ratio had fallen from 0.44% in 1993-94 to 0.25% in 2000-01 and could hardly fall further. Indeed, it was lower by then than at any other time since the mid-1960s.

[7] CCIC News Release, *Development Groups Decry Budget Cuts*, March 31, 1995. Although CIDA Minister André Ouellette administered the cuts, it was Finance Minister Martin who set the levels for Canadian development assistance spending.

[8] Brian Tomlinson, T*he Reality of Aid, 2000*, chapter on Canada, see: http://www.ccic.ca/devpolicy.h tm

[9] CCIC, Achieving the Millennium Development Goals: A Role for Canada, brief to the Standing Committee on Finance, October 21, 2003.

[10] CCIC, *Comparison of Cdn ODA to Defence and Federal Program Spending: 1980 to Present*, Chart prepared by the Development Policy Unit, November 11, 2003.

[11] Paul Martin in Mike Blanchfield, "Canada suspends 11 nations' debts," *The Ottawa Citizen*, December 20, 2000.

[12] Canadian Ecumenical Jubilee Initiative, S*ounding the Trumpet: Educating for Jubilee*, 1998, p. 14.

[13] http://www.ceji-iocj.org/English/index.html

[14] CEJI, *A New Beginning: A Call to Jubilee* petition.

[15] CEJI Response to the Cologne Debt Initiative, July 5, 1999.

[16] See: http://www.halifaxinitiative.org/

[17] Jean Chrétien, Speech to a Luncheon of the Canadian Club of Winnipeg, March 25, 1999.

[18] Notes from John Mihevc, CEJI participant in the meeting.

[19] John Dillon, *Church coalition praises Martin for debt moratorium*, Press Release, 19 December 2000.

[20] Joe Gunn quoted in Art Babych, "Put debt moratorium into perspective: Gunn," *The Prairie Messenger*, January 3, 2001.

[21] Interview with Derek McCuish of the Social Justice Committee of Montreal, November 7, 2003. Indeed, in 2000 CEJI was awarded the Canadian Council for International Cooperation's International Cooperation Award for Influencing Public Policy.

SCEP · IGOT
145

PRINTED IN CANADA